SIGNING THEIR
RIGHTS AWAY

Also by the authors

Signing Their Lives Away:
The Fame and Misfortune of the Men Who Signed
the Declaration of Independence

SIGNING THEIR RIGHTS AWAY

The FAME and MISFORTUNE of the MEN WHO SIGNED The United States Constitution

By Denise Kiernan
& Joseph D'Agnese

QUIRK BOOKS

PHILADELPHIA

Library of Congress Cataloging in Publication Number: 2011922694

ISBN: 978-1-59474-520-1

Printed in China

Typeset in Adobe Caslon Pro, P22 Declaration, and P22 Franklin Caslon

Design by Katie Hatz
Illustrations by Robert Carter
Production management by John J. McGurk

Quirk Books
215 Church Street
Philadelphia, PA 19106
quirkbooks.com

10 9 8 7 6 5 4 3 2 1

Contents

IV. New York

V. New Jersey

VI. Pennsylvania

VII. Delaware

VIII. Maryland

IX. Virginia

X. North Carolina

XI. South Carolina

XII. Georgia

Appendix I.
The U.S. Constitution

Appendix II.

A Constitutional Miscellany

Introduction

★ ★

Ask any person to name the single most important day in United States history, and they're likely to answer July 4, 1776. Every year, Americans celebrate the signing of the Declaration of Independence by attending parades and watching fireworks. Most believe that the patriots defeated the British, as though in a football game, and then Americans lived happily ever after in blissful democracy.

Nothing could be further from the truth.

When the war ended in 1783, the United States was governed by the Articles of Confederation. This fairly flimsy compact provided for a one-house Congress, one vote per state, and very little else. True, this Congress had a president, but he didn't derive his power from the people, and he was an intentionally weak figurehead. After all, the last thing the founding fathers wanted was another king.

Within two years, the fledgling United States was on the verge of political collapse. The federal government had no power to tax people, goods, properties, or businesses. That may sound wonderful until you stop to consider all the consequences: The federal government had no revenue and issued no currency. There was no money for raising troops, building ships, or engaging in other activities vital to a nation's self-defense. The country was vulnerable to attack and domination by a host of foreign powers. At sea, American vessels were pirated by foreign ships; their cargo and passengers were frequently held for ransom. On land, British and Spanish factions were arming Native Americans and encouraging them to raid American settlements on the edges of the frontier.

States took matters into their own hands. Nine states had their own naval forces and pursued their own foreign policies. They imposed taxes on goods from other states as though they were dealing with foreign countries. There were no courts to decide

10   *Signing Their Rights Away*

disagreements between states. Private banks were issuing their own currency, but their notes were often distrusted and viewed as IOUs that might never be repaid. Doing business with other states was challenging if not impossible. Seesawing cycles of inflation and deflation were destroying lives. Foreclosures skyrocketed, and banks began seizing the homes of poor farmers with unpaid mortgages. Many wealthy landowners feared a bloody class revolution—or an all-out civil war.

Clearly something had to be done or the nation wouldn't live long enough to celebrate its eleventh birthday. Alexander Hamilton, James Madison, and a host of other bigwigs proposed a "grand convention" at which delegates would gather to revise, debate, and expand the Articles of Confederation. Seventy-four delegates were chosen by their respective states; only fifty-five answered the call, and many of those with skepticism. Patrick Henry, the famed Virginia rebel, refused to attend, complaining that he "smelt a rat." Rhode Island sent no representatives at all.

In May of 1787, the willing participants journeyed to the very same Philadelphia building where the Declaration of Independence had been signed. True, these men had once banded together to fight as brothers against a common enemy, but now they were deeply distrustful of one another. Small states were suspicious of large states. The nation was divided over slavery. Every delegate arrived wanting something—but few were willing to sacrifice anything. In such a contentious environment, reaching compromise would be tough. More than a dozen delegates quit and went home before the convention's end.

The thirty-nine who remained and signed the U.S. Constitution are the focus of this book. *Signing Their Rights Away* introduces you to the remarkable historical figures who jettisoned the limp and lifeless Articles of Confederation for a robust and rigorous document that provided the framework for an enduring system of government (at more than 220 years old, the U.S. Constitution is the oldest functioning constitution in the world).

In the end, these men prioritized the welfare of their country over politics or personal advancement. They fought with great conviction—but they eventually came to understand that no single delegate could walk away with all the marbles. They agreed to compromise for the greater good. Yet, today, despite their heroic labors, most of them have lapsed into obscurity.

They deserve better—if only because their stories are so interesting. At least twenty-two of the signers served in the military—as soldiers, chaplains, administrative officers—during the Revolutionary War. Five were captured and imprisoned by the British. Many lost homes, property, and loved ones to the war. Two died in duels; one attempted suicide.

Most were educated, cosmopolitan gentlemen accustomed to a life of wealth and privilege. Eighteen of the signers were trained in law; the remainder were merchants, plantation owners, and financiers. They represented the views, expectations, and entitlements of the nation's elite. Such men had no problem ignoring the rights of women and slaves when designing their compact for government. Nor were they champions of free white men with meager property. (One signer sought to restrict government service to men with a net worth exceeding $100,000!) Having witnessed intimidation and mob violence at the hands of enemies and patriots alike, many of the signers didn't trust the American public. The idea of granting power to *all* individuals was a fairly radical idea. During debates, many signers repeatedly derided the notion that Josiah Q. Public could serve wisely in the House and Senate, or, heaven help us, the presidency.

But in the end, enough members knew that this attitude did not reflect the principles of the revolution they had just fought. They were gutsy enough to give the "little guy" a shot at power. Anyone could be president, anyone could be senator—even you.

Signing Their Rights Away

So the next time September 17 rolls around, eat a hot dog, watch some fireworks, and celebrate Constitution Day—that fateful date in 1787 when thirty-nine sweaty men dressed in stockings signed their names to the United States Constitution. Remember how they argued, hoped, feared, persevered, and, most important, compromised to create a lasting document that still governs today. July 4 may be remembered as the day the United States was born, but September 17 marks the country's passage into adulthood, laying the groundwork for two centuries of remarkable expansion and spectacular achievements.

A Constitutional Cheat Sheet

★ ★

Here's a short list of words and phrases you won't find in the original United States Constitution: *God*, *black*, *white*, *women*, *slavery*, *all men are created equal*, *pursuit of happiness*, and *separation of church and state*.

If that comes as a surprise, it's probably been a while since you read the actual document. You can rectify this knowledge gap right now: *Signing Their Rights Away* includes an artistic reproduction of the Constitution on the back of the book jacket, as well as a much more legible transcript beginning on page 216. You'll want to read the entire text before proceeding; it's hard to think of another 4,400-word document that has more greatly impacted world history.

The United States Constitution
vs.
The Declaration of Independence

The United States Constitution	The Declaration of Independence
is about 7,500 words long, including all 27 amendments.	is about 1,300 words long.
begins with: *We the people.*	begins with: *When in the course of human events.*
governs Americans today and provides for the executive, legislative, and judicial branches of government.	separated the colonies from the control of Great Britain.
is the document that presidents, soldiers, government officials, and new American citizens must swear to uphold and protect.	does not govern the American people (though its ideals, notably the concept of "life, liberty, and the pursuit of happiness," seem quintessentially American).
was signed by thirty-nine men on September 17, 1787, but was later ratified or accepted by all thirteen states.	was signed by fifty-six men beginning on August 2, 1776, and possibly not signed by the last signer until 1781.

Before we introduce you to the thirty-nine men who signed the U.S. Constitution, we'd like to introduce some of the terms and themes that will be discussed throughout this book. Fair warning: This cheat sheet makes no attempt to tell the full story of the Constitutional Convention; indeed, that job is beyond the scope of this book (though our bibliography recommends several writers who tell this story particularly well). Our focus here is to celebrate the lives of the signers, but you'll need some of the following information to better understand their achievements.

At the time of the Constitutional Convention, the United States was governed by the **Congress of the Confederation**—basically, the congress provided for by the Articles of Confederation. This congress met in New York City, then the nation's capital.

The constitutional delegates gathered in Philadelphia's Independence Hall from May 25, 1787, until September 17, 1787. George Washington (not yet the first U.S. president, of course, but still wildly famous from his role in the Revolutionary War) was elected president of the Convention.

The most debated topic concerned representation—how the various states would receive a voice in the new congress. Generally, large states favored a proposal called the Virginia Plan, whereas small states preferred the New Jersey Plan, and the resulting logjam nearly brought the entire convention to a stalemate.

The **Virginia Plan** proposed that representation in the national legislature would be based on the population of each state—in short, bigger states would get more say. Not surprisingly, this plan was favored by representatives from the most populous states: Virginia, Pennsylvania, and Massachusetts. To a more limited extent, the plan was also embraced by states that hoped to have huge populations in the future, such as North Carolina, South Carolina, and Georgia.

The **New Jersey Plan** was backed by smaller states like Delaware and Connecticut; they weren't willing to sign away the equal voting rights that already existed in Congress. Under this plan, each state in Congress would have exactly one vote, regardless of population or geographic area.

It's likely the entire convention might have ended in failure if shoe-maker-turned-statesman Roger Sherman hadn't proposed what historians now call the **Great Compromise** (also known as the Connecticut Compromise). His solution: The House of Representatives would have proportional representation based on population, and the Senate would consist of two senators from each state. This system is still in use today.

The second most controversial topic of the convention was slavery. States with large slave populations wanted to include slaves in their total populations (thus increasing their power in the House of Representatives). This idea was ill received by states that had already abolished slavery or were planning or hoping to abolish it. The debate was settled by the **Three-Fifths Compromise**, which allowed states to count each slave as three-fifths of a person for purposes of congressional representation. And since some delegates were uncomfortable with even the use of the word *slave*, the document features the more euphemistic phrase "all other persons."

Throughout the convention, James Madison took meticulous notes, so we know approximately how many times each delegate spoke (some were more vocal than others). Along the way, there were many committees and subcommittees. The **Rules Committee** drafted the guidelines that governed the entire convention. The **Committee of the Whole** was a venue for delegates to let loose and debate topics off the record. The **Committee of Detail** reviewed all the notes and votes and created a first draft of the Constitution, which the **Committee of Style and Arrangement** whipped into a final draft. Finally, there were three **Committees of Eleven**, usually made up of one member from all the states attending; these committees tackled various issues as they arose.

The cursory nature of this overview might suggest that the signers of the Constitution marched together toward a unanimous and happy consensus. The truth is far more unpleasant. The men squabbled for four months behind locked doors in an unventilated building where temperatures routinely exceeded ninety degrees Fahrenheit. At one point, an angry George Washington wrote that the men trapped with him in the room were nothing but a bunch of "narrow-minded politicians." (This was meant as an insult; in Washington's day, gentlemen aspired to be statesmen.)

Washington wasn't alone in his frustration. Most signers ended the convention feeling unsatisfied or disappointed. Benjamin Franklin even admitted that the Constitution was far from perfect: "I confess that there are several parts of this constitution which I do not at present approve . . . but I am not sure I shall never approve them." It was an impassioned speech, but not enough to convince all forty-two of the remaining delegates; three refused to put their names on the document.

And once the remaining thirty-nine had signed, the Constitution still needed **ratification**, or approval, from the states themselves. Nine states were required to put the new government into effect, which would allow for the election of a president and Congress. And so the delegates had to return home and promote the new Constitution to their constituents.

In many parts of the country, it was a tough sell. Public discussions were sometimes accompanied by violent outbursts. Many Americans feared that an empowered federal government would reinstate the tyranny (and unfair taxation) of their former British rulers—only this time, the tyrants would be much closer to home. To advance their cause, signers Alexander Hamilton, James Madison, and John Jay published a series of eighty-five essays supporting ratification (known collectively as the **Federalist Papers**).

Delaware was first to ratify the new Constitution (and if you've ever wondered why it's nicknamed "The First State," now you know). It was followed by Pennsylvania, New Jersey, Georgia, Connecticut, Massachusetts, Maryland, and South Carolina. When New Hampshire became the ninth to ratify the document, the Constitution "went live," but the arguments over the new government never ceased. In fact, many of the same arguments continue to this day.

A Constitutional Time Line
Key milestones in the saga of the U.S. Constitution

★ ★

March 1781: The Articles of Confederation becomes the governing document of the United States.

1783: The Treaty of Paris is signed by Britain and the United States, ending the Revolutionary War.

September 1786: The Annapolis Convention. Five states formally request that Congress schedule a meeting to discuss defects in the Articles of Confederation.

February 21, 1787: The Continental Congress calls for a Constitutional Convention.

May 25, 1787: The Constitutional Convention begins in Philadelphia. George Washington is elected Convention President.

September 17, 1787: The U.S. Constitution is signed by thirty-nine delegates.

December 7, 1787: Delaware becomes the first state to ratify the Constitution.

December 12, 1787: Pennsylvania is the second state to ratify.

December 18, 1787: New Jersey is the third state to ratify.

January 2, 1788: Georgia is the fourth state to ratify.

January 9, 1788: Connecticut is the fifth state to ratify.

February 6, 1788: Massachusetts is the sixth state to ratify.

April 28, 1788: Maryland is the seventh state to ratify.

May 23, 1788: South Carolina is the eighth state to ratify.

Signing Their Rights Away

June 21, 1788: New Hampshire becomes the ninth state to ratify. With nine states on board, the Constitution takes effect as the governing document of the United States.

June 25, 1788: Virginia becomes the tenth state to ratify.

July 26, 1788: New York becomes the eleventh state to ratify.

March 1789: The Congress of the United States meets for the first time under the U.S. Constitution.

April 30, 1789: George Washington is sworn in as first president of the United States under the U.S. Constitution.

September 1789: The Supreme Court of the United States is established under the Constitution.

November 21, 1789: North Carolina becomes the twelfth state to ratify.

May 29, 1790: Rhode Island finally ratifies. The Constitution is in effect throughout the entire United States.

1791: The Bill of Rights (Amendments I–X) is ratified.

The Signers of the U.S. Constitution

These biographies are arranged in the order in which the men signed the constitution—from north to south. The only exception is George Washington, who, as head of the convention, signed first.

I. New Hampshire

John Langdon

★ ★ ★ ★ ★ ★ ★ ★ ★ ★ ★ ★ ★

The Signer Who Picked Up the Tab

BORN: June 25 or 26, 1741
DIED: September 18, 1819
AGE AT SIGNING: 46
PROFESSION: Merchant,
   shipbuilder, politician
BURIED: Old North Cemetery,
   Portsmouth, New Hampshire

★ ★ ★ ★ ★ ★ ★ ★ ★ ★ ★ ★

man possessing that rare combination of great wealth and a willingness to share it, John Langdon went from the sea to the battlefield and very nearly to the vice presidency. One of the Constitution's best-regarded signers has a list of accomplishments that far outweighs the credit he's received for them in modern times. Take it from James Madison, the so-called Father of the Constitution, who described the delegate from the Granite State as a "true patriot and a good man."

Langdon was raised in and around Portsmouth to a family of prosperous farmers. Portsmouth was a major seaport, and, once Langdon's basic elementary education was out of the way, he apprenticed with a merchant. He sailed on a cargo ship to the West Indies and established his own firm. His fortunes grew quickly.

Many of his fellow wealthy merchants were more likely to side with their wallets than with the revolutionary cause, but Langdon was decidedly anti-British. In 1774, two years before independence was declared, he helped colonists storm a British fort and made off with the munitions before the royal governor could get his hands on them. In 1775, he entered New Hampshire politics and served as speaker of the assembly. In 1776, he was elected to the Second Continental Congress. There, his merchant background landed him on the committee that helped develop the first Continental Navy. He left in early 1776 to fight in his colony's militia and operate as New Hampshire's marine agent.

Once back home again, Langdon started a shipyard and began work on a continental frigate, the *Raleigh*. He also oversaw the building of the country's first warship, the *America*. In 1777, he built the *Ranger*, whose command was given to the legendary John Paul Jones, the new nation's first naval officer. (The *Ranger* had the distinction of being the first warship ever to fly the American stars and stripes.) That same year Langdon married Elizabeth Sherburne, and the couple had one daughter who survived to adulthood.

Langdon's largesse was perhaps most influential in the summer of 1777 during the Bennington campaign, which prevented British general Burgoyne from working his way down the Hudson River. This achievement also paved the way for victory in the crucial battle of Saratoga. Langdon offered his militia—and his money—to both. "I have a thousand dollars in hard money," Langdon said. "I will pledge my plate for three thousand more." He also offered to sell off his "seventy hogsheads of Tobago rum" (around four thousand gallons). He was willing to give all this and more "in the service of the state."

After the war, Langdon built a stunning house in Portsmouth. In 1785, he served a one-year term as governor of New Hampshire, a post he would hold another three times throughout his life. He was serving as Speaker of House in the New Hampshire legislature when he received his invitation to the Constitutional Convention; the only problem was that his state wasn't willing to send him. Some believe that New Hampshire was too broke to pay the bill; others claim they just doubted the crazy convention would accomplish anything. Whatever the case, Langdon had to fork over the money himself, and pay for delegate Nicholas Gilman as well. The two men didn't reach Philadelphia until July, long after the convention had started, but better late than never.

They had been sorely missed. The debates over representation were already well under way, as smaller states like Delaware and New Jersey were feeling pushed around by delegates from big states like Virginia and Pennsylvania. They hoped new voices from New Hampshire would add credibility and volume to their arguments.

Langdon was active at the convention and reportedly spoke more than twenty times. His experience as a financier of military operations may have contributed to his belief that a strong central government would make it easier for the new country to defend itself. He "saw no more reason to be afraid of the central government than of the state governments."

"The general and state governments are not enemies to each other," he said, "but different institutions for the good of the people of America. As one of the people, I can say, the National Government is mine, the State Government is mine. In transferring power from one to the other, I only take out of my left hand what it cannot so well use, and put it into my right where it can be better used."

Upon returning to New Hampshire, Langdon worked to secure ratification, but convincing his colleagues back home was no easy task. In February of 1788, he wrote to George Washington to express concern that ratification might not win the necessary votes. Fearing the worst, Langdon had the vote postponed until June; with the extra time, he was able to convince several people on the fence to hop over to his side. The gambit worked, and in June of 1788

New Hampshire became the ninth state to ratify the Constitution, officially putting the Constitution in effect.

The next year, Langdon had the honor of supervising the first presidential electoral vote, making him America's first president *pro tempore*. He tallied the votes and then wrote a note to George Washington, informing his fellow signer that he had been elected as the first president of the United States.

Langdon remained active in New Hampshire politics (serving as governor and in the legislature) but declined all offers to move into the national spotlight. As president, Thomas Jefferson offered him the post of Secretary of the Navy, but Langdon turned it down. When, a few years later, presidential candidate James Madison offered the vice-presidential candidacy, Langdon declined that post as well.

John Langdon lived to be seventy-eight years old (no small achievement at the time), and although he was exceptionally generous in financing the nation's war, such contributions appear not to have threatened his prosperous way of life. George Washington was quoted as saying that Portsmouth had many fine houses, but "among them, Col. Langdon's may be esteemed the first." If you travel today to that picturesque seaside city, you may still visit Langdon's stately Georgian mansion and surrounding gardens.

★ ★ ★ ★ ★ ★ ★ ★ ★ ★ ★ ★

Nicholas Gilman

****

The Most
Handsome Signer

BORN: August 3, 1755
DIED: May 2, 1814
AGE AT SIGNING: 32
PROFESSION: Merchant,
   politician
BURIED: Exeter Cemetery,
   Exeter, New Hampshire

****

Politics can be ugly—especially when you're pretty. Nicholas Gilman, the blond-haired, blue-eyed delegate from New Hampshire, suffered plenty of abuse from his colleagues because of his handsome features and cocky attitude. But look at it another way: if you were handsome in an age when most people sported rotting teeth, pronounced small-pox scars, and countless other afflictions, you might ooze overconfidence, too.

Gilman was born in Exeter to a family that figured prominently in the settling of New Hampshire. (His boyhood home, known as the Ladd-Gilman House, is open to visitors.) Like his father and grandfather, who served in the French and Indian War, Gilman left the family general store at age twenty to enter the military, accepting a post as an administrative officer in a New Hampshire regiment that saw action at

Ticonderoga, Saratoga, Monmouth, and, in 1781, the decisive battle of Yorktown—regarded as the last major conflict of the war. After the death of his colonel, young Captain Gilman was selected by George Washington to determine the number of British troops that would be surrendered by the defeated General Cornwallis.

Upon the death of the Gilman family patriarch, in 1783, the last year of the war, his three sons inherited various slices of his business. The oldest was bequeathed the ships; the youngest, Nathaniel, was left the general store; and middle son Nicholas received a modest inheritance of cash and land. Casting about for a career, Nicholas chose politics. In 1786, he was selected by his home state to serve in the Congress of the Confederation, but something about him rubbed fellow politicians the wrong way. Maybe it was his lack of political experience; maybe it was his less-than-stellar attendance; maybe it was the way he carried on like he owned the place. His colleagues referred to Gilman with the derisive nickname "Congress"—as in, "How's it going, Congress?" or "Fancy a pint at the pub afterward, Congress?"

Yet, despite his unpopularity, Gilman was chosen by his state to attend the Constitutional Convention in 1787. Why would New Hampshire send a man few believed was up to the task? One likely answer is that they didn't *want* to change the federal constitution, and so they sent someone who couldn't possibly accomplish anything. In fact, New Hampshire wasn't even willing to cover the costs of Gilman's trip, and fellow delegate John Langdon generously picked up the tab. The two men arrived at the convention in July, after most of the important decisions had been made.

At thirty-one years old, Gilman likely felt overwhelmed upon arriving at the convention. When you're surrounded by some of the greatest legal and political minds in the states, good looks don't count for much. Georgia delegate William Pierce (who ultimately didn't sign the Constitution but penned some pretty wicked thumbnail descriptions of his fellow delegates) noted that "there is nothing brilliant or striking in [Gilman's] character." Another contemporary described him as a "young man of pretensions; little liked by his colleagues." Gilman's lack of participation certainly didn't help matters. If you scan the meticulous records kept by James Madison, you will find not one word uttered by him during the entire convention. No wonder a modern historian unhesitatingly characterizes Gilman as "mediocre."

We would argue that Gilman redeemed himself by promoting the Constitution to his fellow citizens. The day after signing, he wrote to a friend to say that so much was riding on it being adopted by the states. According to him, the document would decide "whether we shall become a respectable nation or a people torn to pieces by commotions and rendered contemptible for ages." His enthusiasm helped ensure New Hampshire's place of honor as the ninth state to sign, upon which the U.S. Constitution became a binding document.

Under the new government, Gilman continued his service as a U.S. representative, serving in the House for seventeen years. In 1802, at age forty-seven, he failed in his bid for the Senate. Also around that time, he squabbled with his older brother, John Taylor Gilman, who was running for reelection as governor of New Hampshire on the Federalist ticket. Gilman threw his support behind his sibling's opponent, a member of Thomas Jefferson's Democratic-Republican party.

It always helps to have a handsome man on your side. John Taylor Gilman lost the election, and New Hampshire welcomed its new governor, John Langdon, the same man who had paid the younger Gilman's way to Philadelphia eighteen years earlier, on the eve of a more perfect union. As a reward for his loyalty, the party swept Gilman into office as senator. He served nine years but died suddenly while on the road during his second term. He was fifty-eight years old and left behind no immediate family.

An interesting footnote: despite his celebrated good looks and a resume that would have made any debutante swoon, Gilman never married and is one of three bachelor signers of the Constitution.

II. Massachusetts

Nathaniel Gorham

★ ★ ★ ★ ★ ★ ★ ★ ★ ★ ★ ★

The Signer Who Considered a Monarchy

BORN: May 27, 1738
DIED: June 11, 1796
AGE AT SIGNING: 49
PROFESSION: Merchant
BURIED: Phipps Street Burying
    Ground, Charlestown,
    Massachusetts

★ ★ ★ ★ ★ ★ ★ ★ ★ ★ ★ ★

Change the nation and die a wealthy man, and you've got a decent shot of entering the history books. Change the nation and fall into financial ruin—as Nathaniel Gorham of Massachusetts did—and, well, your chances for posterity diminish greatly.

In the here-today-gone-tomorrow annals of American history, tales of great fortune and unexpected impoverishment are not uncommon. But what makes Gorham's tale so unique is that his ruin was aided by the ratification of the very document he worked so hard to create.

Unlike most of his fellow signers, Gorham grew up in a background we'd describe today as middle class. As a child he lived in Charlestown, Massachusetts, where his father operated a packet boat used to deliver mail, among other things. Gorham attended the local public school and then left his home to apprentice as a merchant in New London, Connecticut, where he worked for his keep. Later, he returned to Charlestown to set up his own shop, a mercantile firm, and at age twenty-five he married Rebecca Call, with whom he had nine children.

Like many successful businessmen with good-guy reps and friendly, approachable demeanors, Gorham decided to enter politics. He started out in 1771 as a public notary and became a member of his colony's legislature. The revolution heated up early on in Massachusetts, and Gorham was committed to the patriot cause. In 1774 he became a member of a rebel legislature, where he helped establish the framework for a government that would assume control after the royal governor was booted out. During the Revolutionary War, Gorham served on the Board of War, from 1778 to 1781, and in 1780 he attended the Massachusetts constitutional convention, where his state created its own constitution, one whose draft has been largely attributed to John Adams.

As the war was winding down, the former colonies were still testing the waters of their newfound yet tenuous unity. From 1782 to 1783, Gorham attended the Congress of the Confederation. He returned in 1785 and was elected its president in 1786. This position was, at the time, the highest a person could hold in the nation. Thus, Nathaniel Gorham, the packet boater's son, was "President of the United States in Congress Assembled," which, under the Articles of Confederation, was the closest thing the nation had to a president.

The experience shaped Gorham's views considerably. In 1786, Shay's Rebellion—a violent uprising among poor farmers deeply in debt and angry about the state of the new American government—took place in Massachusetts. This rebellion had a profound effect on many powerful men, including Gorham, who believed that more citizens would revolt if the national government wasn't strengthened. The Articles of Confederation just weren't cutting it.

But Gorham wasn't completely confident that the country could reach a better way to govern via the people—so, as a backup plan, he wrote to Prince Henry of Prussia to ask if he would be interested in serving as king of the United States. This proposal was not nearly as strange as it might seem; in formulating a government for a new nation, it was only natural to look to Europe as a model. But the prince declined, and his close friend Friederich von Steuben quipped, "As far as I know the prince, he would never think of crossing the ocean to be your master. I wrote to him a good while ago what kind of fellows you are; he would not have the patience to stay three days among you."

The next year, when Gorham arrived in Philadelphia for the Constitutional Convention, his accomplishments and popularity had preceded him. He was elected chairman of the Committee of the Whole, essentially making him the number two man, behind George Washington, who was president of the convention. It's believed that Gorham had a perfect attendance record throughout the convention and offered his opinion on a variety of subjects. He suggested a six-year term limit for senators and opposed Gouverneur Morris's insistence that only property owners should have voting rights. "The people have been long accustomed to this right in various parts of America," Gorham said, "and will never allow it to be abridged. We must consult their rooted prejudices if we expect their concurrence in our propositions."

Though he hailed from the fourth most populous colony, Gorham expressed concern that the smaller states might get lost in the representation shuffle. He was in favor of redrawing state lines so that populations would be spread evenly among the colonies, a zany idea that didn't gain much traction among his fellow signers.

Perhaps Gorham's most significant contribution came on the last day of the convention, when he proposed increasing the number of representatives in the House to 1 for every 30,000 citizens (instead of 1 for every 40,000, the figure then under consideration). Before the motion could be debated, the usually reticent George Washington voiced his support—and when George talked, people listened. This change became the very last alteration made to the

Constitution before the delegates added their signatures. (If only Gorham could see America now: the average population in a congressional district has ballooned from 30,000 to 700,000.)

After the Constitution was signed, Gorham urged his colleagues back in his home state to ratify the new document. The idea of an enlarged and empowered central government was a hard sell in Massachusetts, that hotbed of revolution. The vote passed by an extremely narrow margin, and Gorham's hopes of becoming a representative in the new government were dashed. Instead, the state chose Declaration of Independence signer Elbridge Gerry, a delegate who attended the Constitutional Convention but ultimately refused to sign the document.

It was the beginning of Gorham's spectacular decline. Like many of his cosigners, Gorham saw great promise (and the possibility of great wealth) in land speculation. He and his business partner, Oliver Phelps, invested in six million acres in an area of western New York that had been ceded to Massachusetts. They bought the parcel for the bargain-basement price of roughly £300,000 (about $1 million), payable in three installments. But their estimated costs were based on the 1787 value of Massachusetts "scrip," a certificate that was exchangeable for cash at a later date.

Unfortunately for Gorham, the new government guidelines established by the Constitution were about to transform the economy. As Treasury secretary Alexander Hamilton worked to establish a central financial system (and pay off the country's old debts), the value of old securities rose dramatically. Gorham and his partner now owed roughly four times as much on their land contract as they'd originally estimated. The two men went bust, as did countless others in similar situations.

Just a few short years later, in 1796, Gorham died from "apoplexy," or most likely a stroke. You can visit his grave in Charlestown, the Boston neighborhood that is also home to the end of the Freedom Trail, Bunker Hill, and the USS *Constitution*.

The Signer Who Always Ran (and Never Won)

BORN: March 24, 1755
DIED: April 29, 1827
AGE AT SIGNING: 32
PROFESSION: Lawyer
BURIED: Grace Episcopal
    Churchyard, Jamaica, Queens,
    New York

★ ★ ★ ★ ★ ★ ★ ★ ★ ★ ★ ★

Rufus King was the Ralph Nader of early American politics—every few years he would run for vice president or president, and every time he would lose. But these ambitions didn't surface until late in his life, long after he'd helped shape the United States Constitution.

When King was born in 1755, his coastal hometown of Scarborough was part of Massachusetts (it's now a part of Maine). He was the son of a wealthy merchant, a staunch Tory who had defended the Stamp Act. In 1766 local patriots ransacked the family's home, and in 1774 they intimidated the elder King at his house. One historian claims that this event led to the old man's death a year later, in 1775, and instilled in Rufus a love of order and reason.

At the encouragement of his loving but firm stepmother, young

Rufus worked hard in school and was rewarded with admission to Harvard College. Afterward, he served briefly in the Continental Army during the Revolutionary War. One morning, during a break in the fighting in Rhode Island, King was sitting at breakfast with his superiors. Cannon fire broke out, and King left his place to investigate. Another soldier, an officer named Henry Sherburne, wandered in for breakfast and took King's spot at the table. At that moment, a cannonball smashed through the window, landed underneath the table, and crushed every bone in the officer's foot. His leg had to be amputated, and poor Sherburne wore a wooden limb for the rest of his days. Lucky King later told friends, "If this had happened to me on the field, in active duty, the loss of a leg might have been [bearable], but to be condemned through all my future life to say I lost my leg under a breakfast-table, is too bad."

By the time he arrived in Philadelphia for the Constitutional Convention, the thirty-two-year-old King was a brainy Massachusetts legislator and Congressman whose gift for speechmaking, the history books would have you believe, allowed him to trade law for politics forever. (Don't kid yourself: an inheritance from his father—and his marriage to Mary Alsop, a wealthy sixteen-year-old New York socialite—meant he could have underlings manage his business and mercantile interests for the rest of his life.) A handsome five-foot-ten man with a sweet high-toned voice, he outshone his convention colleague Nathaniel Gorham and became the de facto spokesman for the state of Massachusetts and the larger group of so-called big states, which included Pennsylvania and Virginia.

King was a logical man, and he knew a good argument when he heard one. At first, he was adamantly opposed to tinkering with the Articles of Confederation, but fine speeches by other delegates won him over. He became an ardent supporter of a strong Constitution for the sake of the union. In one of his more famous speeches on the convention floor, he argued that the states under the Articles may have seemed appealingly *sovereign*, until you realized that they were also *deaf* and *dumb*: they could not effectively communicate with foreign nations upon whom they relied for trade. They were also completely vulnerable to attack, because they had only limited resources to raise troops and defend themselves. "A union of the States is a union of the men composing them, from whence a national character result to the whole," King was quoted as saying by unofficial note taker James Madison.

King detested slavery and lobbied hard before the convention to prevent the spread of "that peculiar institution" in the largely unsettled lands north of Ohio. He argued that slavery distorted national politics; it gave the South an unfair advantage over the North, both in the production of goods and in population. This stance made him unpopular with some southern delegates, but he didn't care. The nation was divided not so much into big and small states, he insisted, as it was into North and South. Prescient words.

After signing the Constitution, King promoted the document as the nation's last best hope for a strong union. This message was a hard sell in fiercely independent Massachusetts, but the state finally became the sixth to ratify. King hoped to become one of the first Massachusetts senators under the new Constitution, but his personal life was undermining his political aspirations. Since marrying a New York socialite in 1786, he was spending more and more time away, and his political cronies viewed him as an outsider. In 1788, at the urging of Alexander Hamilton, King extinguished the last relic of his Massachusetts life—his law practice—and moved to New York for good. He immersed himself in politics there and was elected to the Senate a year later (beating out Declaration of Independence signer Lewis Morris, among others).

King was reelected to a second term in 1795 but resigned to accept an invitation by President Washington to be U.S. minister, or ambassador, to Great Britain. He served in this post under the country's first three presidents, returning in 1803 to launch a series of runs at the executive office. He twice ran for vice president under his old convention colleague, Charles Cotesworth Pinckney. The duo lost in 1804 to Thomas Jefferson and George Clinton and, in 1808, to James Madison and George Clinton. In 1816 King launched a third campaign, running for president against James Monroe, but lost that bid as well. ("Lost" is something of an understatement. King and his running mate, John Eager Howard of Maryland, were obliterated, 34 electoral votes to 183.)

But his political career was far from over. King enjoyed two more terms as a senator and offered some stirring remarks on slavery when Missouri was being considered for statehood. The nation was already divided between "slave states" and "free states," and King waged a valiant battle to make Missouri one of the latter. In a famous 1820 speech (attended by whites and free blacks), he spoke of how he could not comprehend slavery. "I have yet to learn that one man can make a slave of another," he said. "If one man cannot do so, no number of individuals can have any better right to do it." These were stirring words, but he lost the fight. Much of the northern land that was part of the Louisiana Purchase, then dubbed the Missouri Territory, would be slave-free, but Missouri ended up a slave state, all courtesy of the political agreement known as the Missouri Compromise.

King bid farewell to the Senate forever when President John Quincy Adams asked him to serve yet again as ambassador to Great Britain. Now seventy years old and slowing down, King happily sailed for London, where he had a merry old time, until he fell ill and asked to be relieved of his duties. Two years later, he died at his estate—King Manor in Queens, New York—at the age of seventy-two. Today that estate is open to visitors.

* * * * * * * * * * * *

III. Connecticut

The Signer Who Lived the Longest

BORN: October 7, 1727
DIED: November 14, 1819
AGE AT SIGNING: 59
PROFESSION: Lawyer
BURIED: Christ Episcopal
    Church Cemetery, Stratford,
    Connecticut

* * * * * * * * * * * *

When William Samuel Johnson arrived in Philadelphia in June 1787, people expected big things. At age fifty-nine, this eminent lawyer with dark, smoldering eyes was one of the elder statesmen of the convention; he had earned two diplomas from Yale as well as honorary degrees from Harvard and Oxford. His reputation as an intellectual heavyweight preceded him, and everyone addressed him deferentially as "Dr. Johnson." And yet, he remained surprisingly quiet while the framers hammered out the Constitution, contributing not as much as his fellow Connecticut delegates. Why was he so silent? As his story shows, Johnson was nothing if not cautious.

He was the son of a prosperous, educated clergyman from Strat-ford, Connecticut, who instilled a deep love of learning in his

"Sammy." Despite his father wanting him to become a preacher, the boy pursued law instead. He ended up becoming a prosperous attorney in Connecticut, at a time when many lawyers found it hard to earn a living. He married a wealthy young woman named Ann Beach, whose dowry enlarged his fortune considerably. (He would later tell one of his sons that "marrying well" was "the most easy and agreeable method" of getting ahead.)

Johnson was drawn into politics in 1765 during the Stamp Act controversy, when Americans objected to the levying of an unpopular new tax on all paper products. Everyone seemed to be losing their heads except Johnson, who wisely covered his bases. He spoke out against the tax . . . and then applied to be one of the tax collectors! He was a clearheaded, moderate thinker: just because he considered the taxes unwise didn't mean they wouldn't have to be collected. Johnson's neighbors must have respected his judgment. Rather than string him up, in October 1765 they sent him to the Stamp Act Congress in New York, where he and men from nine colonies tried to develop a coherent response to Parliament's action.

Johnson was rewarded for his middle-of-the-road stance with an invitation to represent Connecticut in London in 1766. This position was a lofty one; every colony had an "agent" in the great city of the Empire. (Ben Franklin was Pennsylvania's agent at the same time.) These agents did not vote, but they were responsible for presenting the views of the colonists to lawmakers. Over time, Johnson came to respect British politics and the stability offered by their system. He returned home in 1774 with big career plans, but the American Revolution dashed them all to pieces.

During the war, Johnson tried to do the impossible: he wanted to remain completely neutral. He had friends who were patriots, he had friends in Parliament—so why should he have to pick sides? Some historians estimate that 15 to 20 percent of the white male colonists were loyalists; 40 to 45 percent were patriots. That means the remainder of colonists—a figure as high as 35 to 45 percent—were neutral, seriously conflicted, or in need of convincing. Johnson may have been on the fence, but he sure wasn't lonely up there.

Johnson's experiences during the war shed light on the difficult position of Loyalists and neutrals during the eight-year conflict. He declined invitations to attend the Continental Congress and refused to lead men in his colony's militia, even though he held the rank of colonel. Instead, he worked for peace, and he was twice arrested by patriots after trying to negotiate between the two sides. He finally quit the Connecticut Legislature, because he felt they had embarked on a treasonous course of action. Barred from practicing law, he and his family were forced to live off savings. But once the war was over, Johnson returned to favor among his neighbors. Towns still needed lawyers and thinkers, after all, and he was one of the best.

Johnson was reticent about attending the Constitutional Convention, but his delegation was active and he never missed a meeting. He lent his support to the Great Compromise and addressed the convention about the wisdom of this decision. He also chaired the Committee of Style and Arrangement, which finalized the language of the document.

When it came time to ratify the Constitution in Connecticut, Johnson was a persuasive salesperson. He insisted that the United States as everyone knew it would cease to be without this powerful new Constitution. "Our commerce is annihilated," he told one group of Connecticut residents. "Our national honor, once in so high esteem is no more. We have got to the very brink of ruin; we must turn back and adopt a new system." He admitted that the document was far from perfect, but he added, at last, "If we reject a plan of government, which with such favorable circumstances is offered for acceptance, I fear our national existence must come to a final end."

It was rare for this cautious old lawyer to utter such a strong opinion, and perhaps legislators in Connecticut knew that Johnson meant business. Regardless, his state became the fifth to ratify the Constitution, and afterward Johnson served as one of Connecticut's first two senators. He was, at age sixty-one, the oldest man in

Congress. He stayed only a few years and then resigned to throw himself into his lifelong passion, nurturing the small college in New York that would one day become Columbia University.

It was a long, lustrous life, and he even remarried at age seventy-four, a few years after the death of his first wife. When he finally died, in 1819, Johnson was ninety-two years old, the oldest of any signer of the Constitution.

* * * * * * * * * * * * *

Connecticut

Roger Sherman

The Signer Who Knew How to Compromise

BORN: April 30, 1721

DIED: July 23, 1793

AGE AT SIGNING: 66

PROFESSION: Cobbler, Lawyer

BURIED: Grove Street Cemetery, New Haven, Connecticut

★ ★ ★ ★ ★ ★ ★ ★ ★ ★ ★ ★

*H*ardworking, experienced, and a fashioner of fine footwear, Roger Sherman was a man who knew how to compromise—a skill that not only saved the Constitutional Convention but also gave the United States one of the key elements of its government, then and now.

Sherman is the only founder to sign the four most important documents in the early history of the United States: the Articles of Association, the Declaration of Independence, the Articles of Confederation, and the Constitution. But he was no pampered planter's son sent off to England to study law and buy fancy wigs. No, Sherman was the son of a working farmer and cobbler—one of a handful of signers, including Hamilton and Franklin, who hailed from humble beginnings. He spent most of his youth in what is now Stoughton, Massachusetts. Money was scarce, but the house had plenty of books, and Sherman was a voracious reader. One popular tale—the truth of which pales in comparison to its charm—says that Sherman slaved away making shoes with a book propped open on his work bench.

After his father's death, Sherman headed to New Milford to join one of his brothers, and legend has it that he traveled the more than 150 miles by foot while toting all the tools of his trade. (One can only assume he was wearing comfortable shoes!) Upon arriving in Connecticut, Sherman found work surveying property boundaries. He also opened a store with his brother and found time to publish his very own almanac. In 1749, his childhood sweetheart, Elizabeth Hartwell, moved to Connecticut to marry him.

When one of his neighbors needed help with a legal dispute, Sherman lent a hand, and a local lawyer encouraged him to enter the profession. So the shoemaker passed the bar, and yet another skill was added to his growing resume. Over the years, Sherman worked as a town selectman, justice of the peace, county judge, and state senator. He held some form of public office his entire adult life and was often dependent upon the jobs for his income.

In 1760, Elizabeth died, leaving Sherman with seven children to look after. He moved to Chapel Street in New Haven and opened a bookstore near Yale, an institution he would serve in various roles over the years (the university would later grant him an honorary degree). He also remarried, to Rebecca Prescott, and added another eight children to the Sherman clan.

A moderate patriot who favored nonviolence, Sherman attended both the first and second Continental Congresses, from 1774 to 1781, as well as the Congress of the Confederation, from 1783 to 1784—all while making time to serve as a judge back home. He even held the post of mayor in New Haven. In Congress, Sherman was well respected from the get-go, garnering praise from even the most hard-to-please delegates. Notoriously prickly John Adams considered Sherman a friend and described him as "honest as an angel and as firm in the Cause of American Independence as Mount Atlas." Thomas Jefferson described him as someone who "never said a foolish thing in his life."

In Congress, Sherman contributed to committees on finance (preferring higher taxes to overprinting paper money) and on military affairs. He served on the Committee of Five that drafted the Declaration of Independence, working alongside primary penman Thomas Jefferson as well as Benjamin Franklin, John Adams, and Robert R. Livingston. He also helped draft the Articles of Confederation.

By the time of the Constitutional Convention, Sherman wasn't quite ready to abandon the Articles of Confederation—he just wanted to make a few tweaks, and, more important, he wanted a legislature with the power to enforce the laws. At the convention, he spoke at least 138 times in a New England accent that was, for many delegates, incomprehensible; Sherman was a Connecticut Yankee in a well-bred and well-born court.

In his journals, Georgia delegate William Pierce observed that Sherman's manner might be peculiar, but there was no doubting the man's ability: "Mr. Sherman exhibits the oddest shaped character I ever remember to have met with. He is awkward, unmeaning, and unaccountably strange in his manner. But in his train of thinking there is something regular, deep and comprehensive; yet the oddity of his address, the vulgarisms that accompany his public speaking, and that strange New England cant which runs through his public as well as his private speaking make everything that is connected with him grotesque and laughable: —and yet he deserves infinite praise—no Man has a better Heart or a clearer Head. If he cannot embellish he can furnish thoughts that are wise and useful. He is an able politician, and extremely artful in accomplishing any particular object; —it is remarked that he seldom fails."

Throughout the convention, Sherman was clear about his views. He believed that national government should address defense, foreign treaties, and trade while leaving most other matters to the states. He also opposed long term limits, warning that if politicians stayed in the capital for extended periods, they would start adopting the habits and priorities of other politicians and forget the people they represented. (We're not sure that having two-year terms for representatives has done anything to address this problem.)

For all his concerns about politicians losing sight of their constituents, Sherman was against allowing every citizen to vote. He placed little faith in the average person to make a well-informed decision, saying, "They want [for] information and are constantly liable to be misled." Sherman wanted the president to be elected by the legislature; if he bungled the job, the legislature would have the power to remove him.

Sherman made history by breaking the convention's biggest logjam: the problem of representation. As discussed in the introduction, the convention was divided between large states favoring the Virginia Plan (which offered proportional representation based on population) and small states favoring the New Jersey Plan (which allowed for one vote per state, regardless of size). Sherman's "Eureka!" moment became known as the Great Compromise: there would be two houses, one in which representation was based on population, and the other would be fixed, providing equal representation for every state no matter its size. The deal stuck and the tenor of the Convention changed dramatically, allowing the delegates to move forward together.

After signing, Sherman wrote numerous articles supporting the Constitution for newspapers back home in Connecticut. And this hard-working Puritan didn't stop once ratification was achieved, despite his advancing age (the only signer older than Sherman was Benjamin Franklin). He went on to be a member of the House of Representatives in the first Congress and then worked as a senator, therefore serving in both chambers of the bicameral legislature whose existence he helped ensure. Few men could, *ahem*, fill his shoes.

Fans of Sherman could argue that the cobbler-judge-surveyor-writer-politician should be remembered as a "co-father" of the Constitution, along with Madison, if for no other reason than that the convention might have imploded without him. His famous descendants include editorial guru Maxwell Perkins and actor Perry King (best known for his role on the 1980s television series *Rip Tide*). Sherman was buried at New Haven Green, but his grave was later moved (as has often occurred with the remains of the signers) to New Haven's Grove Street Cemetery.

Connecticut

★ ★

IV. New York

★ ★

★ ★ ★ ★ ★ ★ ★ ★ ★ ★ ★ ★

The Signer Who Died in a Duel

BORN: January 11, 1755
DIED: July 12, 1804
AGE AT SIGNING: 32
PROFESSION: Lawyer
BURIED: Trinity Churchyard,
New York

★ ★ ★ ★ ★ ★ ★ ★ ★ ★ ★ ★

Slight in size but big on brains, the prickly and persevering "Little Lion" is one of the most impressive and controversial framers of the Constitution. His list of enemies was nearly as long as his list of accomplishments, but the latter has certainly stood the test of time, establishing Alexander Hamilton as a major architectural force in the birth of the U.S. government.

Most of his fellow signers hailed from privileged backgrounds. Hamilton, however, was born out of wedlock to a French mother and a Scottish father in the British West Indies. His father split, his mother died, and by age thirteen Hamilton found himself alone in the world. But the boy was sharp. He apprenticed to a merchant in town, but his intellect and ambition craved more. When a great hurricane struck the islands in 1772, he wrote a letter describing it, which ended up printed in the local newspaper. Hamilton's writing was impressive, prompting Nicholas Cruger, one of his bosses, and local Presbyterian minister Hugh Knox to raise funds to send him to America. They packed him off with a bit of money and several letters of introduction. One was addressed to fellow Presbyterian William Livingston of New Jersey, who took in Hamilton for a spell, arranged for his education, and later signed the Constitution with him.

From an early age, Hamilton supported the revolutionary cause. When he was just eighteen years old, he made speeches in support of the Boston Tea Party and established his reputation as a pamphleteer. When the war came calling, it was like a siren's song. He volunteered for the militia and was drafted by the state, with a commission as a captain. He fought in Long Island, White Plains, Trenton, and Princeton, but his most significant assignment came in 1777, when he became one of General George Washington's aides-de-camp. The two men (separated in age by two decades) became fast friends and developed a relationship akin to father and son. (Not surprising since Washington fathered no children, and Hamilton had been abandoned so young.) Although the trusted confidantes later suffered a falling-out, Washington still trusted Hamilton enough to give him command of a battalion of light infantry in Yorktown. There, the young captain led a famous and tremendously successful nighttime bayonet assault on Redoubt 10, five days before the surrender of General Cornwallis.

After Yorktown, Hamilton returned to Albany and to his wife, Elizabeth Schuyler (they had wed the previous year). The Schuylers were a well-connected and politically powerful family in New York, and the marriage gave him access to power and credibility. Both his law practice and his political career took off.

Hamilton attended the Congress of the Confederation and worked closely with Robert "Financier of the Revolution" Morris, who was then the nation's Superintendent of Finance and in charge of establishing monetary policy. Hamilton moved to New York City to set up his law practice, moving on to the state legislature and attending the Annapolis Convention in 1786. In fact, Hamilton wrote the report issued at the end of the Annapolis meetings, calling for the 1787 Constitutional Convention. Hamilton's strong nationalist views were already fixed, and he is considered one of the driving forces behind the convention's existence.

Unfortunately, the rest of the New York delegation was considerably less enthusiastic. Because Hamilton was guaranteed to attend, thanks to his father-in-law's connections, Governor George Clinton also sent John Lansing and Robert Yates—two men opposed to a strong national government. Moreover, Governor Clinton stipulated that at the convention two members of the New York delegation were required for the state to cast a vote, thus ensuring that Hamilton would perpetually be the odd man out.

But feisty Hamilton was always ready for a rumble. He stayed silent for the first few weeks of the convention, but on June 18 he started talking and quickly made up for lost time; he delivered what is considered the convention's longest speech, clocking in at five hours. He claimed that Britain's government was the best in the world (probably not the most propitious time in history to make that case), and he presented his own plan for government, strongly modeled after Mother England. In his proposal, one branch of the legislature would serve for life, as would the chief executive. For all intents and purposes, Hamilton appeared to favor a form of monarchy. He also warned that "the people do not have the intelligence to determine what is right" and wanted restrictions on who would be eligible to vote. He feared, perhaps rather presciently, that "if elections are held too frequently, the people lose interest and do not bother to vote. Then the small number who do bother to vote can control the country."

The plan was neither seconded nor sent to committee.

This cold reception may be what prompted Hamilton to leave the convention at the end of June, returning home to take care of various business matters. His fellow New York delegates didn't last much longer; by July, Lansing and Yates had given up and gone home as well. Hamilton might not have rejoined the convention if he hadn't received a desperate letter from George Washington in August, urging him back to Philadelphia. More nationalists were needed, Washington implored, and so Hamilton reentered the fray. Even though he was then the only member present from his delegation and therefore ineligible to vote, he nevertheless lent his support to the nationalist camp. He also served on the Committee of Style and Arrangement, which created the final language of the Constitution.

Yet even after signing his name to the document—the only delegate from New York to do so and a noteworthy accomplishment in itself—Hamilton's biggest contribution to the cause was yet to come.

Enter Publius. This pseudonymous essayist took to the New York newspapers in a nonstop ratification campaign extolling the virtues of the Constitution. Though the authorship of some of the essays is disputed, it is believed that Hamilton wrote fifty-one of the eighty-five essays, of which seventy-seven were published in the newspapers. The entire collection was eventually gathered as *Federalist: A Collection of Essays*, which has become known more commonly as the Federalist Papers. Ratification passed in New York by a narrow margin of 30-27, and the essays remain a political-science touchstone to this day.

When Washington took office as president, he appointed Hamilton as the country's first secretary of the Treasury (after Robert Morris declined the offer), and in this post Hamilton retooled the nation's entire financial system. He wanted the national government to take over state debts from the war. He wanted a national bank. He wanted the nation to be a force for industry and insisted on building infrastructure to support its growth. He was on a roll.

But these ideas weren't popular with everyone. Many people were still concerned about the federal government growing too powerful, and Hamilton's aggressive policies, some believed, were just making matters worse. No one expressed these views more consistently than Secretary of State Thomas Jefferson, whose constant bickering with Hamilton would lay the groundwork for the two-party political system that exists in the United States to this day.

Jefferson argued that Hamilton didn't understand the plight of the common man, which is plenty ironic, given that Hamilton grew up parentless and penniless while Jefferson was a patrician planter's son. Their supporters tended to divide along class lines, with Federalists (city-dwelling bankers and businessmen) supporting Hamilton and Democratic-Republicans (pioneers and small farmers) supporting Jefferson.

Hamilton wrote a good bit of Washington's famous farewell address before another Federalist, John Adams, was set to take office. Though Hamilton and Adams belonged to the same party, they were far from friends. In the 1800 election, Hamilton blasted Adams in a missive titled "Letter from Alexander Hamilton Concerning the Public Conduct and Character of John Adams." After Aaron Burr, the vice-presidential candidate for the Democratic-Republican Party, leaked a copy to the newspapers, the Federalist Party was divided and Thomas Jefferson waltzed into the White House. No wonder Adams bad-mouthed Hamilton as "a bastard brat of a Scotch peddler."

Of course, this wouldn't be the last time that Hamilton and Burr crossed paths. In 1804, Burr ran for governor of New York against a Democratic-Republican and wanted the support of Federalists. Naturally, Hamilton urged his fellow party members to support Burr's opponent and even wrote newspaper editorials describing Burr as dangerous and untrustworthy. The smear tactics worked. Burr lost the election and was so angry that he challenged Hamilton to a duel. The two-pistol dance with death was on.

The encounter was scheduled for July 11, 1804, on the west bank of the Hudson River, near what is now Weehawken, New Jersey. Hamilton's shot went wide, but Burr's aim was true. A wounded

Hamilton was rowed across the Hudson to New York City and died the next day, July 12, at age forty-nine. Burr fled the city and was charged with murder, though he never stood trial.

If you wish to commune with the spirit of Hamilton, a plaque in Weehawken commemorates the duel. Hamilton is buried in Trinity Church, in the heart of New York's financial district. His house, known as the Grange, is a National Park site in New York City and is open to the public. The home has the notoriety of having been relocated not once, but twice. For its most recent move, the house had to be lifted off the ground, hoisted into the air on a platform of stilts, and transported over the corner of a neighboring church before being rolled to its new location in Saint Nicholas Park in Harlem.

Of course, if you're not in the mood for travel, you can simply head to your local ATM and snag a $10 bill. Hamilton is one of only three nonpresidents (along with Benjamin Franklin and Salmon P. Chase) to be honored on U.S. paper currency.

* * * * * * * * * * * *

V. New Jersey

Wᵐ Livingston

The Signer-Poet

BORN: November 30?, 1723
DIED: July 25, 1790
AGE AT SIGNING: 63
PROFESSION: Lawyer, writer, shipowner
BURIED: Green-Wood Cemetery, Brooklyn, New York

William Livingston may have believed the pen was mightier than the sword, but he was willing to take up both, as needed, throughout his life. A would-be painter who longed to be a gentleman farmer, Livingston set aside his dreams to obey his family's wishes: he went to law school. If his creativity wasn't encouraged, it was never completely extinguished either. He exhibited fresh ideas through his writing throughout the course of a distinguished political career.

The Livingston family was a financial and social powerhouse in New York and beyond. William was born the fifth child (out of nine) on the family's mammoth estate, Livingston Manor, along the Hudson River. He was raised by his maternal grandmother and, when he was only twelve years old, spent a year with a missionary among the Mohawk. His family worked in the mercantile and fur trades, and they believed that experience on the frontier would be good for William, since he might one day take over the business. Later in life he wrote that the experience gave him "a good opportunity to learn the genius, and manners of the natives."

But Livingston didn't want to be a businessman. What he longed to do was study painting in Italy. Then, as now, most parents weren't thrilled with the prospect of sending a child to art school, so they shipped him off to Yale instead. He pursued law and graduated at the top of his class with a command of several languages—and a desire to write. While clerking for lawyers in New York City, he began drafting a series of essays that skewered the legal profession, the Church of England, and, later, the British. He needed a creative outlet, and he had finally found one.

A self-described "ugly-looking fellow"—the man had a ski slope of a schnoz and did himself no favors with his choice of hairstyle— William fell in love with Susanna French, who hailed from a prominent landowning family that had seen some tough financial times. Initially his parents refused to consent to the union, but they came around when William agreed to delay the wedding by three years. These plans unexpectedly went astray, however, when Susanna found herself pregnant; the couple wed in secret and moved in with an aunt. Livingston's family was not pleased. Later, when his father gave gifts of New York City townhouses to his boys, William was the only son who didn't receive one.

Throughout his successful legal career, Livingston kept writing, crafting poems, and railing against the Church of England. He decried the church's attempts to control King's College (Columbia University), which Livingston thought should be a nonsectarian school; when he was offered a position on the school's board, he declined. Eventually, his editorials became so incendiary that his printer refused to publish them. He defended his prose, saying, "I do declare that I never wrote a syllable with a view of censuring the church as such: I have only exposed her unreasonable encroach-ments . . . it was my duty, my bounden, my indispensable duty."

It's no surprise that a lawyer from a prominent family who had a talent for stirring up the pot would find his way into politics. Along with his older brother Philip, William became a member of New York's colonial legislature. But over time he soured on New York politics and moved to New Jersey, where he bought an estate near Elizabethtown (Elizabeth) and built a mansion called Liberty Hall. Shortly after moving in, a young lad who had recently arrived from the West Indies showed up at his door and presented him with several letters of introduction. Livingston took in the young boy and arranged for his education. The kid turned out well—his name was Alexander Hamilton.

In 1774, after the British closed the port of Boston in retaliation for the Tea Party, Livingston wrote letters for the rebel cause and then served in the first and second Continental Congresses. Though active, he hoped for resolution without bloodshed. After leaving Congress, he took a post as a commander of New Jersey militia, but the poet was ill suited for military life. He once wrote, "My ancient corporeal fabric is almost tottering under the fatigue I have lately undergone: constantly rising at 2 o'clock in the morning to examine our lines."

In August 1776, Livingston was elected New Jersey's first governor, a post he would hold for fourteen years, until his death. He replaced the ousted royal governor and loyalist, William Franklin (Ben Franklin's illegitimate son). While Franklin sat in jail, Livingston was exhorting New Jerseyans to set their "faces like a flint against that dissoluteness of manners and political corruption which will ever be the reproach to any people." From that moment on, he was nicknamed "Doctor Flint."

The war was hard on everyone, rich and poor alike, and Livingston was no exception. His home was ransacked, and a bounty was placed on his head. He lost his son John Lawrence, a midshipman, to the conflict. Currency depreciation and the bankruptcy of numerous debtors depleted his savings. But he did own his home, and he used it to shelter soldiers.

As governor, Doctor Flint saw New Jersey through the war and the wobbly, uncertain years that followed. He joined the New York Anti-Slavery Society and, in 1786, successfully worked to forbid the importation of slaves into New Jersey, even though he owned two of his own. He said slavery was "utterly inconsistent with the principles of Christianity and humanity, and in Americans, who have almost idolized liberty, peculiarly odious and disgraceful."

Livingston's feelings about slavery were tested the next year when he attended the Constitutional Convention and served on the committee that reached the Three-Fifths Compromise. A "small-state nationalist," he supported the New Jersey Plan, which was rejected by the convention, and ended up accepting the Great Compromise, which provided for equal representation in the Senate but population-based representation in the House of Representatives.

Livingston signed the Constitution at age sixty-three—the third oldest man to do so—and went back to New Jersey to work on securing a speedy ratification before serious opposition could be organized. (New Jersey was one of only three states to ratify before the end of 1787.) Still governor, Livingston received an honorary law degree from Yale not long before his death. He lost his wife, Susanna, in 1789, and shortly thereafter became sick as well. He died in 1790.

Then his next journey began, for one of the worst things you could do for the fate of your earthly remains was to sign the Declaration of Independence or the U.S. Constitution. Livingston was buried first in a New Jersey Presbyterian churchyard, but a year later his body was moved to a family vault at Trinity Churchyard in Manhattan. In 1844, his body was moved yet again to—*gasp!*—the outer boroughs. Today you can visit his grave at Brooklyn's Greenwood Cemetery. Liberty Hall was never moved and is now a lovely museum on the grounds of Kean University. It is open to the public and is a popular site for weddings, which surely would have made the poet in Livingston smile.

David Brearley

★ ★ ★ ★ ★ ★ ★ ★ ★ ★ ★ ★

The Signer Who Proposed Erasing State Boundaries and Starting Over

BORN: June 11, 1745
DIED: August 16, 1790
AGE AT SIGNING: 42
PROFESSION: Lawyer
BURIED: St. Michael's
    Episcopal Church Graveyard,
    Trenton, New Jersey

★ ★ ★ ★ ★ ★ ★ ★ ★ ★ ★ ★

Pennsylvania half its size? Little Rhode Island three times bigger? Was this the key to equitable representation among the first thirteen states? We'll never know—but it's certainly one of the strangest ideas floated at the Constitutional Convention, and it comes courtesy of David Brearley.

Brearley was born in Spring Grove, New Jersey. He was one of five children in a family that owned land but wasn't particularly wealthy. Nevertheless, he received a good education and attended the College of New Jersey, a little school that was later known as

Princeton, although he left before graduation to pursue law. Things moved along rather nicely for young Brearley. By the age of twenty-two, he had been admitted to the New Jersey bar, moved to Allentown to start his own practice, and married Elizabeth Mullen, with whom he would have four children.

Then came the Revolutionary War and all the skirmishes proceeding from that first shot heard 'round the world. Brearley was always a stalwart patriot in a state that had its fair share of loyalists, and his outspoken manner didn't win him any popularity contests with then-royal governor William Franklin (the illegitimate son of Electric Ben). His dedication to the patriot cause resulted in his arrest for treason, but his capture was short-lived. Before he could be hanged, a group of like-minded revolutionaries sprung him loose from the clutches of the British.

Brearley continued to fight and took up arms in the New Jersey militia, where he rose from the rank of captain and eventually become a colonel. It was a time of hardship and hard work. He lost his wife, Elizabeth, in 1777; he fought in various battles throughout New Jersey and Pennsylvania; and he helped draft the New Jersey Constitution, which would govern the state after the royal governor, Franklin, was ousted.

In 1779, Brearley became chief justice of New Jersey and soon found himself involved in the groundbreaking trial of *Holmes v. Walton*, a case involving a smuggler, John Holmes, who was tried and convicted of dealing contraband. During the war it was tempting to sell goods to the British—they paid with real hard cash, not depreciating paper money and promissory notes that were the oh-so-weak currency of the colonies. But there was a problem with Holmes's trial: he had been convicted by a jury of six men, rather than the usual twelve, as dictated by British Common Law. The appeal to the state's supreme court landed in Brearley's lap, and he dismissed all charges—a hugely unpopular decision but a necessary one, in Brearley's opinion, because the conviction violated the state's constitutional right guaranteeing trial by jury. Because Holmes hadn't been granted a full jury, the trial was null and void. This decision would be cited in years to come and referenced as one of the first to establish the power of a supreme court to determine whether a law is constitutional, known as the principle of judicial review.

The year after this famed decision, Brearley was given an honorary master's degree from Princeton, despite never having officially finished his studies. He was plenty popular around New Jersey but not quite popular enough to become governor, a post he sought three times (and lost, each time, to William Livingston).

With a new wife, Elizabeth Higbee, whom he married in 1783, three more children, and an admirable legal career, Brearley was a natural delegate to the Constitutional Convention. He was, in fact, the very first delegate elected from any of the colonies. He didn't speak much during the proceedings in Philadelphia that summer—but if there was any topic that got his knickers in a wad, it was bigger states attempting to control Congress at the expense of smaller states. According to James Madison, Brearley felt that "the substitution of a ratio . . . carried fairness on the face of it; but on a deeper examination was unfair and unjust." He noted that proportional representation in both the House and the Senate would give a more populous state such as Virginia sixteen votes, while sparsely populated Georgia would cast a measly one.

"What remedy then?" Brearley asked. "One only: that a map of the United States be spread out, and that all the existing boundaries be erased, and that a new partition of the whole be made into thirteen equal parts." Some reports say that Brearley was serious, but others claim he was merely taking his beliefs to an extreme to make a point. In the end, he put his support behind William Paterson's New Jersey Plan, which gave each state one vote, no matter its size.

Later Brearley embraced the principles of the Great Compromise, though he insisted on capping the size of the House at sixty-five members. He got his wish, but not for long; as time passed and the nation's population increased, more states and more people necessitated more representatives. By 1929, the House had grown to 435 members—and has remained at that number ever since, despite not even coming close to the minimum representational standards set out by the framers in 1787. (Today, movements in the United States seek to return to the ratio of 1 representative per 30,000 citizens first outlined in 1787. Among other obstacles, the Capitol would require a serious overhaul to accommodate all those people. New York City alone would require 267 representatives!)

Brearley happily signed the Constitution and was president of the state ratification convention in New Jersey. In addition to continuing his legal practice, he acted as grand master of the New Jersey Masons, found time to help work on the Book of Common Prayer for the Episcopal Church, and served as the state vice president of the Society of the Cincinnati, a veterans organization founded after the Revolutionary War. It is named for the Roman Cincinnatus, a farmer who fought bravely but famously returned home after battles to tend his fields, passing up greater power and spoils of war. George Washington was regarded as the Cincinnatus of the West and served as the group's first president-general. The organization still exists today.

Washington appointed Brearley the U.S. district judge of New Jersey in 1789, a post he held for less than a year before dying, at age forty-five. If you visit Trenton, you can stop by to see the memorial dedicated to Brearley at the Grand Lodge of Masons before heading to St. Michael's Episcopal Church, where the famed framer is buried.

* * * * * * * * * * * * *

The Son of a Door-to-Door Salesman

BORN: December 24, 1745
DIED: September 9, 1806
AGE AT SIGNING: 42
PROFESSION: Lawyer, judge
BURIED: Albany Rural
    Cemetery, Menands,
    New York

* * * * * * * * * * * *

The framers of the U.S. Constitution represented the nation's elite—wealthy, privileged men who had much to gain from the creation of a strong, stable government. Only a handful came from modest backgrounds, and William Paterson was among them. The son of a peddler who sold pots and pans going door to door, he would one day rise to become a governor, a senator, and a justice of the U.S. Supreme Court.

Paterson's parents emigrated from northern Ireland to America a few years after he was born, eventually settling in Princeton (literally across the street from the famous college, which was then in its infancy). His parents saved enough to send their first-born son to the school, and he did them proud by staying long enough to acquire a master's degree. He went on to study law with Richard Stockton, a local man of culture who would one day sign the Declaration of Independence. Young Paterson probably longed to move to Philadelphia, New York, or even Trenton, but unlike his wealthy friends at school, he didn't have the connections to establish himself in a large city. And so he kept to Princeton's farm country; he ended up serving on his colony's supreme court while also running a law practice and working for his father. (Lawyers had yet to pioneer billing software and the $250 hourly rate and so had to supplement their incomes in all sorts of ways.)

Paterson grew into a diminutive, painfully bookish man with a bulbous nose and an aversion for romantic attachments, developing a reputation for being an uptight, friendless workaholic. He disowned family members who borrowed money and didn't repay, censured male friends who married women pregnant with their children, and came down hard in his court judgments on fornicators and debtors. From the bench he railed against publick houses, billiards, and booze. He seemed to fear that society would descend into anarchy unless certain people—namely, himself—imposed order.

And like many people who feel the same, Paterson found his way into politics.

He became immersed in rebel activity in the 1770s, just as the colonies were heating up, and served on the committee that arrested New Jersey's royal governor, William Franklin. Now an attorney general in the new patriot government, Paterson refused to serve in the Continental Congress, claiming he was too busy. Less-charitable historians say that he didn't want to leave New Jersey because— finally—he was making decent money.

In his thirties, Paterson found love not once, but twice. His first romance inspired him to spend long hours writing love letters to his dear Cornelia Bell. In 1779, he installed his new bride in a posh four-hundred-acre estate in New Jersey that had been swiped from a loyalist family and snapped up by Paterson in a bargain sale. But their love would be short-lived, for Cornelia died just four years after their wedding day. But soon he married Euphemia White, one of his wife's girlfriends.

In 1786, Paterson attended the Annapolis Convention and shared concerns that the Articles of Confederation must be revised. This time around, nothing would keep the older, more confident, well-heeled lawyer from going to Philadelphia. Influential men around the nation were already familiar with his writings, political work, and court decisions, and the forty-one-year-old quickly became the voice of the New Jersey delegation and de facto spokesman for so-called small states fearful of being robbed of both their rights and their tax money by their larger neighbors. Early on, Paterson insisted that accepting Virginia's plan for representation based on population was tantamount to tyranny and despotism. He would not be a party to it. He would fight it on the convention floor and do all he could to demolish the measure at home. Instead, Paterson and his small-state confreres presented the New Jersey Plan, which preserved the one state–one vote setup of the Articles of Confederation and merely tacked on a chief executive, to be chosen by that Congress, and a court to settle disputes.

It was a tight, law-and-order plan from a tight, law-and-order man. The small states loved it, because it appeared to preserve the equal voting rights they already enjoyed under the Confederation. The big states hated it, because it required states to be taxed according to their populations: *Oh, so we'll kick in more money, but you'll have equal say over how it's spent? We think not!* The delegates fought over the warring plans for weeks, until Roger Sherman introduced the Great Compromise.

Delighted that the power of the big states would be checked, Paterson left the convention at the end of July 1787 to attend to various business matters. He returned to sign the finished Constitution and

Signing Their Rights Away

supported its ratification. (Though he signed the document "Paterson," his name is sometimes spelled with two *T*s.)

Despite serving as one of New Jersey's first senators, Paterson claimed to hate public life. When his convention colleague William Livingston died in office, he was sworn in as the second governor and, over the next eight years, revised many of the state's laws. He approved the creation of a town named Paterson, which Alexander Hamilton, the nation's new secretary of the Treasury, hoped to build into the country's most powerful manufacturing center by harnessing the power of the city's waterfalls. (The results were mixed, and recent years have not been kind to Paterson the place; today, a large percentage of the city's population lives below the poverty line.)

In 1793, Paterson left the governorship to serve as an associate justice on the U.S. Supreme Court. While performing his circuit-court duties, he famously instructed a jury to render a guilty verdict and then ordered the execution of the ringleaders of the Whiskey Rebellion, an early-1790s uprising against a despised whiskey tax. Washington pardoned the men, thinking Paterson's judgment too harsh; indeed, modern historians call the decision "indefensible." The hard-as-nails judge later declined Washington's invitation to serve as Secretary of State.

In 1803, Paterson was gravely injured when a team of horses went wild and sent his carriage toppling over. He tried to continue his job on the bench, but, with his health shattered, he finally had to step down. He died at the age of sixty while visiting his daughter in upstate New York.

★ ★ ★ ★ ★ ★ ★ ★ ★ ★ ★ ★

Jona: Dayton

★ ★ ★ ★ ★ ★ ★ ★ ★ ★ ★ ★

The Signer Who Stole $18,000 from Congress

BORN: October 16, 1760
DIED: October 9, 1824
AGE AT SIGNING: 26
PROFESSION: Lawyer,
    politician
BURIED: St. John's Episcopal
    Church, Elizabeth,
    New Jersey

★ ★ ★ ★ ★ ★ ★ ★ ★ ★ ★ ★

At the time of the nation's founding, human life could be brutally short. The medications that today allow us to manage conditions like heart disease and diabetes simply didn't exist. The common cold could be a killer. Gout was rampant. And the smallest scrape or cut might lead to an amputation. Knowing that life was precious, people in revolutionary America matured quickly and stepped into adult roles while still very young. All of which helps explain how a New Jersey delegate named Jonathan Dayton came to sign the U.S. Constitution at the tender age of twenty-six.

The youngest signer was born in Elizabethtown, New Jersey, the son of a storekeeper and local politician. At the time of the Revolutionary

War he was studying at the future Princeton University but entered the Continental Army with his father before he could finish his studies. He fought throughout the northeast, from Canada to Pennsylvania, and in 1780 was captured, along with his uncle, during a skirmish in his home state. The pair was released in a prisoner exchange the next year. Young Captain Dayton went on to fight in a famed bayonet attack on Redoubt 10 in Yorktown under the command of his old schoolmate Alexander Hamilton and the Marquis de Lafayette. After the war, Dayton became a lawyer and entered local politics. He married Susannah Williamson, with whom he had two children.

In 1787, the New Jersey legislature chose his father, Elias Dayton, to attend the Constitutional Convention. The elder Dayton didn't want to go, so instead he sent his son. Rumor has it that dad sent junior to Philadelphia to keep him away from the bad influences of misbehaving friends. And with his young son out from under, goes the theory, Papa Elias would be able to focus on running the family business.

Thus, says one historian, Dayton's presence at the convention was regarded as something of an insult to the profound legal thinkers present. One of the more charitable delegates noted that Dayton was "little known; having no other merit than to be the son of a good patriot." Others were more direct, including Georgia delegate William Pierce, who claimed, "There is an impetuosity in his temper that is injurious to him."

In Dayton's defense, plenty of evidence suggests that he was an active member of the convention. According to James Madison's copious notes, Dayton angrily defended the right of small states to an equal say in their future government: "He considered the system on the table [the Virginia Plan] as a novelty, an amphibious monster; and was persuaded that it would never be received by the people." To no one's surprise, Dayton supported William Paterson's New Jersey Plan, but he ultimately came around to the Great Compromise. He joined fellow delegates in signing the Constitution, went home to help push through ratification, and embarked on a promising career that would see him become one of New Jersey's first U.S. representatives and senators. He had been elected Speaker of the House by the age of thirty-four.

Like many a rising star, Dayton had a weakness: investing in real estate and other astounding speculative ventures. He was "notorious from Boston to Georgia," wrote one historian who studied Dayton's wheeling and dealing. "The deeds of other men in Congress were scarcely known beyond the circle of their respective states, but the speculations of this man have rung throughout the western world." A month after the convention, Dayton teamed up with a syndicate of other men to buy up tremendous amounts of land—one million acres—on the Miami River in Ohio. The plan was to lure New Jersey farmers out west and sell them the land at a profit. (Dayton, Ohio, was named by its first settlers in his honor.) But when the syndicate ran into trouble paying back the borrowed money, Dayton sweet-talked creditors into more favorable terms. Unlike fellow signers Robert Morris and James Wilson, he managed to avoid debtor's prison.

Still, his decline continued. He next invested $18,000 worth of congressional cash into yet another land speculation deal. Although Congress tracked down the money and Dayton returned it, his reputation was forever tarnished. Few people trusted him—except the man who would lead to his downfall.

Aaron Burr befriended Dayton when the two were students at Princeton. The friendship blossomed when Burr became vice president under Thomas Jefferson, but then events took an outrageous turn. Burr allegedly lured Dayton into a strange scheme to invade Spanish-held lands in the western part of the continent. The motives for the plot are sketchy even today; many speculate that Burr wanted to carve out his own mini-empire in the west. Whatever the reason, Dayton did lend his friend some money, creating a financial paper trail that proved to be his undoing. (It's not clear if he intended to participate in Burr's plan.)

When Thomas Jefferson got wind of the scheme, he ordered the capture of all alleged conspirators. Dayton was arrested for treason in 1807 and posted bail but was never brought to trial. Burr stood trial. Despite Jefferson's angry exhortations to Chief Justice John Marshall to convict, Burr was found not guilty.

Yet, guilt by association was enough to ruin Dayton's already tarnished political career. He continued to serve in the New Jersey legislature but never again stepped foot onto the national stage. He became something of a pathetic figure later in life. Active in various veteran organizations, he was known for wearing tricorn hats and colonial dress long after they'd gone out of style. "The last of the cocked hats," people called him.

When the dear old Marquis de Lafayette returned to the United States at the invitation of President James Monroe for a tour of the nation he'd helped liberate, Dayton was high on the list of men who feted him. Incessant carousing exhausted Dayton and wrecked his health. He died in 1824, just before his sixty-fourth birthday. He is buried in the churchyard of St. John's Church in Elizabeth, but you'll never find his plot there. When the church was rebuilt in 1860, elders saw fit to erect the new structure right over his grave.

★ ★ ★ ★ ★ ★ ★ ★ ★ ★ ★ ★

VI. Pennsylvania

Franklin (signature)

BORN: January 17, 1706
DIED: April 17, 1790
AGE AT SIGNING: 81
PROFESSION: Printer,
    scientist, philosopher
BURIED: Christ Church Burial
    Ground, Philadelphia,
    Pennsylvania

After nine years of serving in France as his nation's minister, Benjamin Franklin returned to Philadelphia with a golden sedan chair—a carriage designed to be hefted by four strong men. Franklin was pushing eighty years old and suffering from gout, and he had no patience for walking the muddy streets of Philadelphia. Instead, prisoners on loan from the local jail carried him aloft, seated in his sedan, as if he were a god.

And though he was no deity, he was undoubtedly the world's best-known American. In his eight decades, Franklin had stood in the presence of five kings and summoned thunderbolts from the

heavens. He was a printer, a publisher, a writer, a scientist, a philoso-
pher, an inventor, and a philanthropist, all in a single lifetime.
Franklin had none of Thomas Jefferson's patrician advantages, and
yet this self-made man ended his life wealthier, more famous, and
more adored than all his contemporaries. Even today, he remains the
most famous of the founding fathers.

Franklin began life as a lowborn son of a Boston candlemaker.
He ran away from his first job to Philadelphia, where he prospered
at the press of a printer. He traveled to England to apprentice and
returned to print his own newspaper, *The Pennsylvania Gazette*, and
an annual, *Poor Richard's Almanack*. These publications were chock
full of maxims you still hear uttered today, including, "A penny saved
is a penny earned" and "Early to Bed, and early to rise, makes a Man
healthy, wealthy, and wise." *Poor Richard's* soon became the second
most popular book in the country (after the Bible). Farmers craved
its planting advice, and all colonists wanted its useful calendar. The
pamphlet was cheap and written for ordinary people. While many
signers condescended to the common man (John Adams called the
populace "rabble"), Franklin was sympathetic—even though, by age
forty-two, he was rich enough to leave his business in the hands of
a partner and devote himself to philanthropic work and the building
of a new nation.

He improved life in Philadelphia by creating the first American
hospital, library, and volunteer fire department. He worked to create
the academy that would later grow into the University of Pennsylvania, and he traveled throughout the colonies seeking to better the
colonial mail system. In recognition of his efforts, Parliament appointed him postmaster general. He also cranked out inventions,
including such useful items as the Franklin stove, the lightning rod,
and bifocals.

Franklin is so closely associated with Philadelphia and early
colonial life that it's somewhat shocking to realize that he spent
nearly three decades living in Europe. Following his early visit to

England as a printer's apprentice, he returned in 1757 for another ten years to serve as an agent of Pennsylvania. He became embroiled in a scandal concerning leaked antirebel letters written by the royal governor of Massachusetts; these letters were stolen for Franklin by another future signer of the Constitution: Hugh Williamson, of North Carolina.

Back in America in 1775, Franklin decided that he supported a total break with the motherland. He helped draft the Declaration of Independence and became the document's oldest signer, at age seventy.

In the fall of 1776, Franklin left once again for Europe, hopping a ship on a secret mission to beseech France for troops and funds to fight the war. Franklin charmed the pants off France, which kicked in cash and forty-four thousand troops, effectively clinching the war for the Americans. Franklin spent the rest of the Revolution in France (while his finances, unlike those of his fellow signers, tripled) and helped craft the U.S.–Britain peace accord, known as the Treaty of Paris, which he, among others, signed in 1783.

Though Franklin had never been a great speaker and the niceties of law eluded him, the organizers of the 1787 convention knew that his presence would lend the debates an air of respectability. If Washington and Franklin—then serving as Pennsylvania's governor—took part, it would send a signal that the convention was far more important than whatever Congress was working on in New York, which was then the seat of government.

But old age had done a number on Franklin. He was then eighty-one years old. Everything ached. He often propped up his gout-swollen feet and napped through the deliberations. When too tired to speak, he would pass notes to his friend, legal logician James Wilson, who read them aloud in his distinctive Scottish accent.

It's not clear that Franklin contributed any great ideas toward the creation of the Constitution. What we do know is that he told humorous stories and parables, which lightened the mood, broke logjams, and often prompted the angry delegates to resume conversations. On one memorable occasion, he interrupted a heated discussion by signaling a motion to hire a local preacher to lead the delegates in prayer every morning. It was fine idea, but it forced the delegates to confront an embarrassing fact: the U.S. government was so broke, it couldn't afford the fee! Had wise Franklin made the motion to shame the men into negotiating in earnest? Or was he tossing out random ideas to keep from dozing off?

But his endless storytelling made some delegates nervous. The deliberations were supposed to be kept completely secret—if Americans learned that delegates were constantly bickering, rumors might spread that the union was unraveling. Believing Franklin could keep a secret about as well as a thirteen-year-old blogger, the convention assigned two men to tail him each night and ensure he didn't blab publicly about the day's events.

Franklin supported a unicameral, or single-house, legislature, and a weak president, or possibly a council of men to act together as chief executive. He disliked the idea of entrusting a single person with so much power, and he was against paying politicians for their services. Handsome wages would attract only greedy, narrow-minded men who lusted for power and money, he said. In time, such good-for-nothings would raise taxes in a ceaseless bid to milk the government dry.

But when Charles Pinckney, a delegate from South Carolina, suggested that only men with a net worth of at least $100,000 be allowed to serve in government, Franklin protested. He argued that some of the biggest rogues he'd ever met were wealthy men, and he warned that immigrants might stop moving to the United States because it would be perceived not as a land of opportunity, but as a domain of the rich.

On another occasion, when delegates were clashing over how best to represent the states in Congress, Franklin told a story of a woodworker building a table. What happens when the pieces of wood don't match up perfectly? he asked. The craftsman takes a little from each piece until they dovetail beautifully; he doesn't give up until he makes it work. The message was obvious: *Do likewise, gents, or we are doomed.* Shortly after, delegates from Connecticut proposed the Great Compromise.

At the end of the convention, before the document had been signed, Franklin was invited to make the closing remarks. He labored over a beautiful speech, which was read by James Wilson. The speech unwittingly handed delegates the message they would parrot to their constituents back home: *This document may not be perfect, but it's the best we can do.*

"I cannot help expressing a wish," added Franklin, "that every member of the Convention who may still have objections to it, would with me, on this occasion, doubt a little of his own infallibility, and to make manifest our unanimity, put his name to this instrument."

The thirty-nine signed, his words still ringing in their ears.

A final anecdote: Franklin spent much of the convention scrutinizing George Washington's chair, the back of which was decorated with the motif of a sun, with shafts of light radiating outward. Franklin couldn't shake the chair from his mind. Did it depict dawn or dusk? He could not decide. On the last day of the convention, after the men had signed the document, he told the delegates of his little dilemma and concluded, "But now at length I have the happiness to know that it is a *rising* and not a setting sun!"

The oldest signer of the U.S. Constitution lived to see the document ratified and his friend Washington elected as the first president of the United States. In 1790, Franklin became the first signer of the Constitution to die. He passed away at age eighty-four and is buried in Philadelphia.

* * * * * * * * * * * *

The Signer Who Was Ruined by Drink

BORN: January 10, 1744
DIED: January 20, 1800
AGE AT SIGNING: 43
PROFESSION: Merchant, soldier, politician
BURIED: Trinity Lutheran Churchyard, Lancaster, Pennsylvania

★ ★ ★ ★ ★ ★ ★ ★ ★ ★ ★ ★

In revolutionary times, it was commonly believed that alcohol gave people strength—and our founding fathers needed all the strength they could get. They drank nearly every day—morning, noon, and night. Some historians estimate that the average person living in revolutionary America guzzled six gallons of pure alcohol every year (today that number is probably closer to two).

Stephen Hopkins, a signer of the Declaration of Independence, was famous for imbibing rum in congressional chambers. Luther Martin, a brilliant Baltimore attorney who ultimately did not sign the Constitution, gave one of his most famous, albeit craziest, convention speeches while absolutely tanked. Yet both men ended life with their reputations relatively intact.

So what happened with Thomas Mifflin? How could this constitutional delegate (and future governor of Pennsylvania) be ruined by alcohol? The answer lies in the mores of the time. For while heavy drinking was acceptable in revolutionary America, flagrant public drunkenness was not. And, alas, Mifflin's frequent tipsiness made him an easy mark for political enemies.

Born in Philadelphia, Mifflin was the son of wealthy merchant parents. He studied at the future University of Pennsylvania, clerked at a local business, toured England and France, and opened a store in Philadelphia with his brother. He became active in politics while still in his twenties and identified strongly with patriots, who were in the minority in Pennsylvania. Though affluent all his life, he seemed to have the common touch and formed a strong bond with the state's poorer citizens, farmers and laborers alike. One writer described him as "very popular and handling with a surprising ease the hundred-headed monster known as the people." But he was also a brooding, temperamental man who longed to contribute to his country's formation. At the first Continental Congress, a delighted Mifflin was among the group of men who chose Washington to lead the Continental forces. Later, Mifflin himself was picked as the general's aide-de-camp. As he kissed his beloved wife, Sarah, good-bye and dashed off to war, his Quaker brethren voted to boot him out of the meetinghouse for bearing arms.

Mifflin fought with distinction at the battles of Long Island, Trenton, and Princeton. He was eventually promoted to the rank of major general but spent much of his time, at Washington's request, working as the army's quartermaster in charge of locating supplies and outfitting troops. Though he was allowed to collect a commission on goods he bought and sold, and his sharp mind for logistics and mercantile background made him an obvious choice for the post, Mifflin likely detested the job and considered it a waste of his talents. He preferred to be out in the field or raising morale among the troops and is credited with persuading many soldiers to remain in the service. Ironically, after the disastrous seizure of Philadelphia by the British in 1777, Mifflin tried to resign his job, claiming he was too ill to continue. Historians think he just wanted to ditch the outfitter gig. Yet, he remained in the military and ended up working for the Board of War, the Congressional committee in charge of army matters. That post no doubt bored him to tears as well.

At some point, Mifflin grew fed up with being sidelined and involved himself with the notorious Conway Cabal, a plot to oust and replace Washington with another military hero, General Horatio Gates. When Washington's supporters learned of the plan, they demanded to see the financial records Mifflin had kept while quarter-master, insisting that he had misused government money in what one historian calls a "highly unethical, albeit legal way." Unfortunately, Mifflin's records were a mess. Washington wanted to court-martial him for insubordination, but Mifflin escaped the general's wrath by ignominiously resigning from the military. To silence his foes, in 1782 Mifflin published his "economic autobiography" in a local newspaper, which has provided historians with a fascinating account of one man's astute accumulation of wealth—through real estate, ships, and army commissions—during wartime.

Cut to 1783. The war is over. George Washington, now regarded as nothing short of a saint, returns to resign his commission before Congress. Who should Washington see sitting in the exalted seat of power, as president of Congress, but his old nemesis, Thomas Mifflin. In an absurdly flowery speech, Mifflin ate crow and thanked Washington for, um, winning the war and stuff.

Mifflin was still president of Congress when the nation formally ended the Revolutionary War. After leaving Congress, he was active in Pennsylvania's legislature and even served as the state's president, a precursor to the governorship. It's true that he went to the Constitutional Convention in 1787, but no one has found any record of his participation, beyond seconding a motion and signing the document on September 17. In 1790, he was elected the first governor of the Keystone State by an incredible margin of 10–1. Some wags later gossiped that he'd bought off the election by pandering to his beloved lower-class voters. One can picture the "handsome rotund" Mifflin glad-handing the rabble in Philly's taverns, tankard in hand. He stayed in office nine years, during some of the worst times in the state's history. He presided over the horrors of the yellow fever epidemics and later sent Pennsylvania's militia into the state's frontier territory to quell the 1794 Whiskey Rebellion. In raising troops for the militia, he addressed the common people and invoked the document forever linked with his name: "Are you willing to serve your country; to save your Constitution, and to assist in securing from anarchy, as you did from despotism, the freedom and independence of America?"

His three terms as governor were marred, however, by accusations of bad personal behavior. Claiming to be sick, Mifflin often skipped important meetings. Oliver Wolcott, a son of a signer of the Declaration of Independence and the nation's new secretary of the Treasury, confided to a friend, "The governor is an habitual drunkard. Every day, and not infrequently in the forenoon, he is unable to articulate distinctly." (Ah, no wonder Mifflin was always described as having a "hearty claret color or rather ruddy complexion.") This sad truth might have been easier to live down had it not been accompanied by more charges of embezzlement. Apparently, Mifflin had dipped into public funds, withdrawing money from a Pennsylvania bank for his personal use, only to repay the funds when the truth was uncovered.

In 1799, Mifflin closed out his last term in the new seat of the state government—Lancaster, Pennsylvania. He accepted duties in the state house but didn't live long to perform them. He was dead within a month, at the age of fifty-six. A lavish spender who dodged creditors toward the end of his life, he left behind an estate so squandered that he had to be buried at public expense.

★ ★ ★ ★ ★ ★ ★ ★ ★ ★ ★ ★

The Signer Who Went to Debtors' Prison

BORN: January 31, 1734
DIED: May 8, 1806
AGE AT SIGNING: 53
PROFESSION: Merchant,
   banker, land speculator
BURIED: Christ Church,
   Philadelphia, Pennsylvania

★ ★ ★ ★ ★ ★ ★ ★ ★ ★ ★ ★

Known to history as the "Financier of the Revolution," Robert Morris was a tremendously successful merchant, banker, broker, and fund-raiser. But for all his efforts to keep the fledgling United States and its army from going broke, he wasn't able to manage the same for himself.

One of the few immigrant signers, Morris was born in Liverpool, England. He came to America with his father and quickly established himself as a merchant, prospering as a partner in his own firm in Philadelphia called Willing and Morris. He married Mary White, and together they had five children. Being a wealthy merchant and

Pennsylvania

banker with one of the biggest shipping firms in the colonies made Morris an unlikely candidate to aid the revolutionary cause. There was money to be made, after all. He may have been frustrated with the Stamp Act of 1765, for example, but he wasn't so upset that he wanted to revolt. He did, however, sign nonimportation agreements, promising his fellow patriots that he would not trade in British goods, a gutsy stance for anyone who traded with the Crown.

As he became more involved with the patriot cause, Morris's firm began importing arms and ammunition for Congress. Sent to the Continental Congress in 1776, he was relied upon for his financial prowess and connections. He worked on the Secret Committee of Commerce, which acquired foreign goods for the military, paying for them with in-kind shipments of goods from the colonies. Soon after entering Congress, however, the pesky issue of whether to declare independence from Britain arose. Morris thought the timing was all wrong. He was not alone.

Pennsylvania was divided. Although Morris did not want to vote for independence, he also didn't want to prevent the motion from passing. So, on the day of the big vote, he simply played hooky. After the resolution passed, he signed the Declaration of Independence, becoming the only Pennsylvania signer who could have voted for independence but chose not to. Later, Morris explained why he continued to serve his nation even though he disagreed with its choice to become independent: "I think that an individual who declines the service of his country because its councils are not comfortable to his ideas, makes but a bad subject; a good one will follow if he cannot lead." The next year, he even apologized for not supporting independence.

To finance the American Revolution, Morris wheeled, dealed, begged, borrowed, and then some. Most historians agree that without the three-pronged team of Franklin wooing the French, Washington fighting the war, and Moneybags Morris securing the cash, the Union Jack would still be flying high over the states. Larger-than-life Morris was socially skilled and had a talent for charming folks out of their money. He had connections in the financial world that Congress lacked, and copious personal credit to boot. When times were desperate, he even dipped into his personal savings.

When the troops needed food, ammunition, and dry boots, when Congress didn't have any real credit to speak of, Morris was the man. Washington wrote to Morris directly when he was banked on the Delaware waiting to cross, with precious few supplies on hand. Morris brought out the checkbook, and Washington took the Hessians to the cleaners. Later, Morris secured funding for Washington's Yorktown campaign, which helped end the war. The two men would be friends for life.

The resilience of Morris's fortunes, even in wartime, was regarded as impressive by some, suspicious by others. In 1779, he was accused of war profiteering, but a congressional hearing cleared his name. Despite the setback, he was appointed by Congress as the nation's superintendent of finance in 1781, and he got to work revamping the nation's money system. Assisted by cosigner and friend Gouverneur Morris (no relation), Morris set the withering finances of the colonies back on track, established new procedures for supplying the military, and founded America's first government-incorporated bank, the Bank of North America, considered to be the model for Alexander Hamilton's later creation, the Bank of the United States. Morris resigned his post in 1784 to focus on business, returning to Pennsylvania politics in time for the Constitutional Convention.

Morris, like Washington, was a strong nationalist and thought the Articles of Confederation should be revamped or replaced. But his behavior at the convention was surprisingly discreet. On the first day, he officially nominated Washington to be convention president but then kept mum for the rest of the proceedings. It may have been that he preferred back-room politics. Ever the socialite, Morris hosted Washington at his home in Philadelphia, and they would receive other delegates after hours. There were dinner parties, invitations to Morris's estate outside town, and, of course, frequent trips to the pub. Perhaps Morris was more interested in discussing his views over pints rather than on public record.

He did regard the resulting document, with all its perceived flaws and controversy, as the work of "plain, honest men," and he was happy to sign it. Washington offered him the job as first secretary of the Treasury, but Morris passed it up, choosing instead to serve as a senator to the first Congress. He supported Hamilton's financial system, which drew inspiration from Morris's term as superintendent of finance.

Like many of his fellow delegates, Morris was swept up in the land speculation craze of the late 1780s. He—alone and with partners—bought and sold millions of acres of land throughout the colonies and the territories west of the established states. At one point, his land holdings were estimated to be worth roughly $2 million (yes, those are eighteenth-century dollars). But Morris let his ambitions get away from him. Much of what he bought was purchased with public securities, and when the values of those securities increased, Morris's finances took a dive. Immigration dried up, and so did interest in frontier property. He was upside-down on his loans with no way to dig himself out and not a federal bailout in sight. The great financial mind of the Revolution was arrested and sent to Philadelphia's Prune Street debtor's prison. He left behind his family as well as an unfinished mansion on Chestnut Street that became known as Morris's Folly. (It was later torn apart for scrap.)

While Morris served his time, his old friend Washington stopped by to visit and even dined with him. His friend Gouverneur Morris secured an annuity for his wife, Mary, so that she could support herself; that same money helped the couple when Morris was later released. He spent the end of his remarkable life in obscurity, dying bankrupt and all but lost to history, although his contributions to the origins of the United States cannot be contested. In 1878, long after Morris was gone, the nation honored him by placing his portrait on the first $10 silver certificate.

Morris's other Philadelphia home, on Market Street, is also long gone, but the site—across from the Independence Visitor's Center—is now preserved as an African American heritage site and is open to the public. When Philadelphia was the nation's capital, Morris rented the home to George Washington, who is known to have kept nine slaves there while he was president. A statue of Morris stands just east of Independence Hall, and he is buried at nearby Christ Church.

Despite his early misgivings, Morris lent his signature to all three of the most important documents of the time: the Declaration of Independence, the Articles of Confederation, and the Constitution. Connecticut's Roger Sherman is the only other man to have done so.

* * * * * * * * * * * *

Gea. Clymer

* * * * * * * * * * * *

The Signer Whose Home Was Destroyed by the British

BORN: March 16, 1739
DIED: January 24, 1813
AGE AT SIGNING: 48
PROFESSION: Merchant
BURIED: Friends Meeting
  House Cemetery, Trenton,
  New Jersey

* * * * * * * * * * * *

George Clymer was a quiet, unassuming moneybags with no desire to serve in public office. But the new nation could not have survived were it not for men of his keen intelligence—and deep pockets—working behind the scenes.

Clymer cut a handsome figure, with his aquiline nose, wispy hair, and fine features. The son of a sea captain, he was orphaned at an early age and raised by an aunt and uncle. Luckily for him, his uncle, a buddy of Benjamin Franklin, was a wealthy and cultured merchant. Clymer followed in his uncle's footsteps, devouring every book in the man's library and then raking in the cash from shrewd business deals in the import-export business.

He gave people the impression of being a cool cucumber—some would even mistake him for being lazy—but his doctor and friend, Declaration of Independence signer Benjamin Rush, said that nothing could be further from the truth. Behind that polished exterior, Rush claimed, was a warm, open-hearted man who had great affection for the patriot cause. Clymer would even support the rights of people vastly different from him, specifically Native Americans and immigrants, on whose behalf he would later negotiate peace and rights settlements. As early as 1773, when Clymer was in his mid-thirties, he chaired the board that organized the Philadelphia Tea Party—virtually unknown to most Americans today—along with other smaller tea parties that took place around the same time; these events pressured merchants who were licensed to sell English tea to renounce their posts as royal consignees.

Also in 1773, Clymer saw some service as captain in a corps of volunteer troops nicknamed the "Silk Stockings," because so many members were from well-heeled, blueblood families. The group used its military might to force local merchants to stop selling British tea. Clymer further distinguished himself with another important war-time service to his new country: fund-raising. He raised money for military supplies of all types—corn, flour, gunpowder, and tenting materials. And he backed the Revolutionary War by exchanging some of his own gold and silver—the safest of commodities—for risky Continental currency that wouldn't have been worth the paper it was printed on had the revolution ended in failure. He even served as Continental treasurer during the first year of the war.

One of six signers of the Declaration of Independence who also signed the Constitution, Clymer, along with his family, suffered at the hands of the British during the war. When the Redcoats blitzed through Philadelphia in the fall of 1777, Congress fled, leaving Clymer (and fellow signer Robert Morris) to manage paperwork and keep the financial wheels of government turning. In September

1777, British troops destroyed Clymer's country estate outside Philadelphia as Clymer's wife, Elizabeth Meredith, and their children hid in nearby woods and watched the destruction. Thankfully, the damage did not inhibit Clymer's ability to earn a living—or to lend others money. Twenty years after the Declaration was signed, he was back to his old bankrolling ways, bailing out the University of Pennsylvania from possible bankruptcy, creating banks, and establishing art academies, among other philanthropic ventures.

Clymer was not a lawyer and didn't say much at the Constitutional Convention. His name appears in Madison's records only a few times, motioning or voting on matters relating to taxation, slavery, and navigation. During a discussion of the three-fifths compromise, he objected, for instance, to the word *slaves* being used in the Constitution; the framers ended up changing the word to the euphemistic "all other persons," as if to sweep the entire issue under the rug.

Clymer did serve on important business committees during the summer of 1787. He was a man who believed that those sent to Congress should "think *for* and not *with* his constituents." True to that dictum, he often ignored his own constituents' wishes when they conflicted with what he thought was the smart course of action. That might sound hard-hearted, but most modern members of Congress, if they were honest, would probably agree. It's impractical to ask voters for their opinion on every issue; they vote for the person who will do the best job of representing their interests. In general, Clymer voted at the convention like the man he was—a big shot from a big state.

After the convention, Pennsylvania elected him a U.S. representative to the first Congress; he served out his term and didn't seek reelection. He was, to his core, a behind-the-scenes man and was duly appointed by Washington to handle the management and collection of excise taxes for the new government. He knew goods, he knew business, he knew taxes. But the excise tax on whiskey turned out to be such an unpopular issue (especially in Pennsylvania, site of the

Whiskey Rebellion) that Clymer sickened of the abuse his department received and stepped down. At Washington's request, he negotiated peace treaties with Creek and Cherokee tribes in Georgia.

Upon retiring at age fifty-seven, Clymer continued to stay active in social, charitable, and philanthropic works. In 1806, still smarting from the destruction of his prerevolutionary home, he bought another house, Summerseat, in Morrisville, Pennsylvania, which is still standing and open to the public. He died there in 1813, at the age of seventy-three. He is buried in a Quaker cemetery in Trenton, New Jersey, under a modest stone that hails him as a signer of the Constitution but does not mention that he also signed the Declaration of Independence.

★ ★ ★ ★ ★ ★ ★ ★ ★ ★ ★ ★ ★

Thoˢ FitzSimons

★ ★ ★ ★ ★ ★ ★ ★ ★ ★ ★ ★

The Signer Who Loaned Away His Fortune (and Never Got It Back)

BORN: 1741

DIED: August 26, 1811

AGE AT SIGNING: About 46

PROFESSION: Merchant

BURIED: St. Mary's Roman
        Catholic Churchyard,
        Independence National
        Historical Park, Philadelphia

★ ★ ★ ★ ★ ★ ★ ★ ★ ★ ★ ★

Thomas FitzSimons had a lengthy and impressive resume in the world of finance, but this hard-won experience didn't keep him from losing his entire fortune.

One of seven signers born outside America, FitzSimons emigrated from Ireland to the bustling city of Philadelphia, where his father quickly established a business. FitzSimons wanted to follow in his father's footsteps, so to learn the ropes he clerked in the mercantile business. His professional plans were helped considerably by his love life. After marrying Catherine Meade, who came from a fine family in town, FitzSimons partnered with his new brother-in-law George to become part of the "company" in George Meade and Co. The firm was successful at trading with the West Indies, and FitzSimons quickly established himself as a smart financier.

He was active in the Irish Catholic community and, in 1771, became vice president of the fraternal organization of the Friendly Sons of Saint Patrick. In 1774, Parliament passed the Coercive Acts—legislation that punished American colonists for their role in the Boston Tea Party. One of these acts closed the port of Boston, which made an importer-exporter like FitzSimons shiver in his buckle-shoes. As anti-British sentiment heated up, he became involved with Philadelphia protests and the community began to perceive him as a leader.

What makes FitzSimons's ascent all the more remarkable is his religion: he was Catholic at a time when anti-Catholic sentiment pervaded the colonies. Most colonists viewed Catholics as agents of the papacy. In many parts of the colonies, they were prohibited from worshipping in public, holding office, practicing law, and voting. In fact, to keep Catholics out of public office, colonies would sometimes require new hires to take the so-called religious Test Oath. Doing so as a Catholic often meant denouncing several tenets of the faith (including the sacrament of Communion and adoration of saints).

Yet somehow FitzSimons navigated around these prejudices to become what many believe was the first-ever Roman Catholic elected to a public office in the colonies. His patriotism, combined with his business savvy, earned him spots on Pennsylvania's committee of correspondence (a letter-writing, intelligence-gathering ring established by patriots) as well as a seat on the provincial (or rebel) congress.

FitzSimons helped organize his colony's militia in 1775 and marched to New Jersey to support George Washington's troops in 1776 and 1777. When his days as a captain ended, he continued contributing to the Revolution as a member of the new nation's Navy board and the committee of safety, a military-governmental group of volunteers charged with defending the public. His business provided supplies for the troops and donated thousands of British pounds to the almost-always-broke Continental Army. Yet, despite the war, he kept the cash rolling in.

In the years after the conflict, FitzSimons became concerned about the fiscal health of the colonies, worrying especially about inflation. Working with fellow Constitution signer Robert Morris, he organized the first Bank of North America and served on its board for more than twenty years.

In 1782 and 1783, FitzSimons served in the Congress of the Confederation. He also served on the Pennsylvania Council of Censors, an organization that guarded against violations of the state's constitution, as well as the state legislature. In 1786, he was sent to the Annapolis Convention, the meeting at which the delegates decided that the Articles of Confederation needed a good overhaul.

So when the Constitutional Convention came to pass and the new states tackled the revision of the Articles, FitzSimons was there. He didn't speak much, but there was little doubt about his position. He was a strong nationalist who fell in line with the other businessmen supporting large-state interests. He sided with Gouverneur Morris, who believed that property ownership should be a requirement for voting for Congress. FitzSimons also wanted government to regulate trade and commerce. Not surprisingly, he preferred the Virginia Plan (which favored large states) and opposed the New Jersey Plan (which favored small ones), though he was supportive of the Great Compromise. FitzSimons was one of only two Catholics to sign the Constitution (the other was Daniel Carroll, a cousin of the Declaration of Independence's only Catholic signer, Charles Carroll of Carrollton). Incidentally, his name appears as FitzSimons on the Constitution, but it's been spelled elsewhere as Fitzsimons and Fitzsimmons, depending on who is wielding the pen.

FitzSimons served in the new government as a three-term representative to Congress and was active in the growing Federalist Party. When he was defeated for reelection in 1794, James Madison called it a "stinging change for the aristocracy."

He remained active in finance and philanthropy, serving as president of the Insurance Company of North America, a trustee of the University of Pennsylvania, and several times as the president of the Chamber of Commerce. And he cochaired a big farewell dinner for George Washington when the beloved first president left office. Clearly, no amount of anti-Catholic prejudice could overshadow his mercantile prowess and generous wallet. Not one to forget his roots, he was also a big—if not the biggest—financial supporter of the construction of St. Augustine's Roman Catholic Church in Philadelphia.

FitzSimons was, in other words, well positioned to leave a spectacular legacy to the country—until he was bit by the land-speculation bug. The notion of purchasing lands on the western frontier with devalued securities might seem ill advised in hindsight, but many with money (including fellow Constitution signers William Blount and Nathaniel Gorham) thought it was an excellent gamble. Making matters worse was that FitzSimons, ever the soul of generosity, loaned hundreds of thousands of dollars to friends, including fellow signer Robert Morris. When Morris saw his investments disappear, FitzSimons was dragged down into the fiscal mire as well. He lost his fortunes and died without recouping them.

Upon FitzSimons's death, in 1811, when he was about seventy years old, *The Philadelphia Gazette* wrote that he "was justly considered one of the most enlightened and intelligent merchants in the United States . . . after many and great losses he died in the esteem, affection and gratitude of all classes of his fellow citizens." He is buried on the grounds of St. Mary's Roman Catholic Church in Independence National Historical Park, Philadelphia.

* * * * * * * * * * * *

Jarod Ingersoll

* * * * * * * * * * * *

The Signer Who Couldn't Keep Up with Fashion

BORN: October 27, 1749
DIED: October 31, 1822
AGE AT SIGNING: 37
PROFESSION: Lawyer
BURIED: Old Pine Street
    Presbyterian Church
    Cemetery, Philadelphia,
    Pennsylvania

* * * * * * * * * * * *

What good is a new constitution if you can't take it out for a spin? After the document was ratified by the states, the new Supreme Court began applying its principles to a number of important cases. One decision so enraged Congress that it quickly created a new amendment (the eleventh) to prevent similar decisions in the future. And the man at the center of the action was Jared Ingersoll, a thin-as-a-rail Philadelphia lawyer who had signed the Constitution less than a decade earlier.

Ingersoll was born in Connecticut, the son of a wealthy loyalist lawyer who supported even the most unpopular acts of Parliament, including the Stamp Act. The elder Ingersoll took on the post of tax collector during the mid-1760s. One night, as he was riding on horseback, he was stopped on the road by an angry mob of five hundred patriots who demanded his resignation. With pitchforks and torches waving in his face, he wisely followed their advice and quit on the spot. Soon afterward, he moved his family to Philadelphia.

Young Jared graduated from Yale in 1766 and, for a short time, clerked for his father. Neither father nor son supported the colonists in the Revolutionary War, so they decided that Jared would leave the powder keg behind and go abroad for school. He studied law at London's Middle Temple, a prestigious law school, and then took time to explore Europe, particularly France.

But in 1778 a curious thing happened: Ingersoll returned home and declared himself a patriot. To this day, historians aren't really sure what caused this abrupt political conversion. Was there something in the attitudes of his instructors and fellow students that made him sympathize with the American cause? Had he been persuaded by Ben Franklin, who was then working as a U.S. minister in France? Did he merely mature and view politics differently from his father? Or did he switch sides for a more pragmatic reason? Maybe he was concerned about fitting in with his old friends back home. Whatever the reason, he returned full of disdain for Mother England.

Once back on colonial shores, Ingersoll married Elizabeth Pettit, the daughter of a wealthy merchant, had four children, and settled into the life of a respectable Philadelphia lawyer, even as the war raged around him. Known for his stiff, almost military posture, he was reserved and conservative by nature, but an adroit speaker in the courtroom. "Woe betided the adversary that took a false position, or used an illogical argument, or misstated a fact against him," wrote one of his former clerks. "He fastened upon the mistake with the grasp of death, and would repeat and reiterate and multiply his assaults upon it, until there did not remain a shadow of excuse for the blunder."

And yet when Ingersoll attended the Constitutional Convention in 1787, he scarcely said a word. "There is a modesty in his character that keeps him back," observed Georgia delegate William Pierce. Ingersoll spoke up just once, on the very last day, when he seconded Ben Franklin's motion that the framers sign the Constitution without delay. (Clearly, he was ready to go home.) The document wasn't perfect, Franklin had said, but it was the best they could produce, and Ingersoll agreed.

After the convention, Ingersoll, who believed in a strong national government, landed important legal posts in the Federalist government of Pennsylvania, though he would never rise to the level of Supreme Court justice. In 1791, when he applied to argue cases before the nation's highest court, his application was rejected because of insufficient professional stature. Some historians wonder if government officials weren't rapping him on the knuckles for the sins of his father, or for his own early stance as a loyalist.

Nevertheless, Ingersoll was involved in some landmark Supreme Court cases, including one that inspired the Eleventh Amendment. *Chisholm v. Georgia* concerned a South Carolina man suing the state of Georgia for nonpayment of war debts. Ingersoll, the counsel for Georgia, refused to appear before the court, arguing that the feds had no right to hear the case because Georgia was a sovereign, or independent, state and couldn't be dragged into a case before the Supreme Court. In a 4-1 decision, the Supreme Court rejected his argument, saying that the Constitution did give the high court the right to hear cases brought against states by citizens of *other* states. They might have been willing to hear the merits of Georgia's case, but because the state of Georgia didn't appear, four justices said they had no choice but to decide in favor of Chisholm.

What irritated Americans more than anything was the court's assertion that only the federal government had sovereign immunity from such suits. Because the issue of states' rights was (and still is) a touchy one, Congress immediately proposed the Eleventh Amendment to the Constitution, which specifically prohibits the Supreme Court from hearing cases in which states are sued by citizens of other states. Ratified in 1795, less than a year after it was proposed, the amendment may be one that most Americans never pause to consider, but it became the first passed specifically to overturn a Supreme Court ruling. And to this day it's still debated by legal scholars.

In 1796, while he was attorney general of Pennsylvania, Ingersoll argued and lost another pivotal case, *Hylton v. United States*, the first legal challenge to the constitutionality of an act of Congress. (In the case, the court found that Congress did not overstep its taxing and spending powers when it imposed a $16 tax on carriages.) One of Ingersoll's more infamous cases was his defense of William Blount, a shady Tennessee politician and Constitution signer who was the first person ever to be impeached by the federal government under the Constitution.

When John Adams was about to leave office as president, one of his last official acts was to stack the circuit courts throughout the land with as many Federalist "midnight judges" as possible. Ingersoll was so rewarded for his loyalty, but he declined the post.

Thomas Jefferson's rise to the presidency spelled doom for most Federalists in power, and Ingersoll was no exception. He retreated into private practice for a decade but remained active in the Federalist Party in Pennsylvania. In 1812, he ran unsuccessfully for vice president of the United States with presidential running mate DeWitt Clinton. If you're asking, "DeWitt who?" you already know the outcome. The pair lost, and James Madison was swept into office as the nation's fourth president.

Still, Ingersoll remained active—as attorney general, in Philadelphia district court, and in private practice—almost to the day he keeled over. But it wasn't a love of work that kept him going; he was desperately out of money. Some years back, he had invested in western land with fellow signer Robert Morris, and when those deals proved disastrous, all investors were left looking at empty bank accounts. This likely explains why Ingersoll wore colonial clothes long after they'd gone out of style. While the fashions of the period were transitioning to long pants and tall boots, Ingersoll still fastened his colonial breeches and buckle shoes and dressed in frilly shirts, bowing to the ladies while doffing his old tricorn hat. He died on Halloween day of 1822, at the age of seventy-three.

James Wilson

The Signer-Turned-Fugitive

BORN: September 14, 1742
DIED: August 21, 1798
AGE AT SIGNING: 45
PROFESSION: Lawyer
BURIED: Christ Church,
    Philadelphia, Pennsylvania

★ ★ ★ ★ ★ ★ ★ ★ ★ ★ ★ ★

James Wilson wasn't the first signer of the Constitution to make a few extremely boneheaded financial decisions, but rare is the story that can match the quirky details of his brilliant rise and fall. This astute colonial lawyer went from being a Supreme Court justice to a jailbird to a man on the run. He contributed so much to the founding of the nation—and yet his reputation was quickly erased by colleagues the moment he died, in an effort to sweep his scandals under the rug of history.

Wilson was born in Scotland and studied at not one but three universities before arriving in Philadelphia to seek his fortune. When he soured on a teaching job, he zeroed in on law. Once he was admitted to the bar, Wilson left Philadelphia for Reading, and then Carlisle, Pennsylvania, where he developed a lucrative practice among Scotch-Irish settlers. Since many cases involved land disputes, he absorbed much privileged information about various parcels and soon succumbed to the lure of speculation: with borrowed money, he bought land and flipped it for a profit. In time, he acquired a home, a wealthy wife named Rachel Bird, and a slave, settling into a life he could not have imagined in his homeland. He and Rachel had six children.

Wilson found time to lecture on literature and other topics in Philadelphia. He was among the first intellectuals to argue that Parliament had no authority over the colonies, and he felt that the colonists should look instead to the king as their link to the Empire. Having analyzed Parliament's decision to close the port of Boston in 1774 in response to the Boston Tea Party, Wilson called the act unconstitutional. That was a fascinating leap of logic, because under English law no act of Parliament could ever be considered unconstitutional. Wilson's reasoning was ahead of its time. By presuming to judge whether a piece of legislation was correct, he implied that judges could, and should, second-guess legislators. This concept of judicial review would later become a central tenet of the U.S. legal system.

In Congress, the reserved, somewhat awkward Wilson cut an impressive figure with his six-foot height, his Scottish burr, and his dignified expression obscured behind thick, nerdy glasses. Declaration of Independence signer Benjamin Rush called him a "profound and accurate scholar," continuing rapturously: "His mind, while he spoke, was one blaze of light."

Wilson was a political moderate, though he grew more conservative with each passing year. He was sent to Congress in May 1775 and signed the Declaration of Independence in 1776. But later, when his new state was crafting a constitution that gave power to the citizens, Wilson attacked it. Although he *believed* that the power of any government rested with the people, he acted like a man lacking these beliefs. Eventually, such behavior made him unpopular with his constituents, and they voted him out of Congress in the fall of 1777.

In the years following the signing of the Declaration, Wilson transformed himself from a frontier lawyer into an odious corporate attorney. He also switched from being a Whig—the party that opposed royal power—to a virtual Tory. He even changed his religion; the traditional Scottish Presbyterian converted to the Episcopal faith. He bought a nice townhouse in Philadelphia, invested in land, and defended beleaguered Tory merchants in court. The city's patriots grew to detest him. In the fall of 1779, when inflation was at an all-time high and food was scarce, a mob of angry, inebriated lower-class citizens and militiamen swarmed Wilson's townhouse at Third and Walnut Streets. "Get Wilson!" was their rallying cry. Wilson and his cronies barricaded themselves inside and desperately fired on the crowd, which returned shots. Between three and seven people were killed; as many as nineteen may have been injured. Wilson decided to flee town until emotions cooled. The next spring, the legislature pardoned everyone involved in what was sarcastically called the Fort Wilson incident.

Wilson returned to public life after the war, when others like him—aristocratic in bearing and behavior—were in power. But he seemed to set all that aside when he walked into the 1787 Constitutional Convention. There he was a major force behind the creation of the U.S. Constitution, championing its most democratic principles. Friends with Benjamin Franklin since the days of the Declaration, Wilson sat near the older man and often read aloud Franklin's notes and speeches. At age eighty-one, the once-spry Franklin was too tired to stand and address the delegates.

But Wilson was no mere mouthpiece. James Madison may be credited as the father of the Constitution, but Wilson is often recognized as the number-two man. Not only was he one of the top speakers at the convention (with an impressive 168 recorded remarks), he put forth an idea that is the cornerstone of American government: namely, that a system of checks and balances was required to ensure that the power invested in leaders cannot be abused. Wilson famously showed the delegates a picture of a pyramid. In order for the federal government to be truly powerful, he explained, it must, like a pyramid, have the broadest possible base. In other words, it must have the support of the American people. Again, he argued that judges would act as a check on the legislature by striking down unconstitutional laws. He defended the idea of having one person as the chief executive when delegates insisted that such a practice would lead to the creation of a virtual monarchy. And he insisted that the president should be elected by the American people and not the legislature, as some had suggested. Only then would citizens feel invested in their government.

True to his big-state roots, Wilson supported the idea of proportional representation in Congress. He proposed that senators be elected to nine-year terms. At the time, everyone assumed that the Senate would draw the wealthiest, most educated Americans. Two-year terms were fine for the rabble in the House; but senators needed to serve for a substantial time. The delegates finally settled on six-year Senate terms, rotating so that one-third of the Senate would leave each year; that way, the assembly would always have fresh blood. Wilson served on the committee that wrote the Constitution and may himself have contributed substantial chunks of the text. He signed the document a few days after his forty-fifth birthday, returning home to convince Pennsylvanians to ratify the document.

Wilson expected to be selected as the first chief justice of the Supreme Court—but those hopes were soon dashed. Washington did choose him as the court's first justice, but he was tapped to be an associate, not chief justice (that honor went to John Jay). Around the same time, Wilson became the first law professor at the future University of Pennsylvania.

All might have ended well if Wilson hadn't made a number of ill-advised business decisions. Chief among them was buying land tracts in western New York, Pennsylvania, and Georgia—all on borrowed money. If he had lived in the twenty-first-century, Wilson would have been at the head of the housing-bubble pack, gobbling up more land than he could afford. It's estimated he held one million acres in his portfolio, not to mention factories, ships, and ironworks. He and his investors, among them signer Robert Morris, had a scheme to import immigrants to settle the land, thereby earning a handsome profit. While on the high court, he was hounded by critics and almost impeached because he promoted laws written to help—who else?—land speculators.

How could someone so smart be so clueless? When the money stopped flowing, Wilson owed hundreds of thousands of dollars that he couldn't repay. Creditors hounded him to the point that he confided to a friend he was being "hunted like a wild beast." He became a liability on the high court because he couldn't travel to certain states to hear cases—he risked being arrested by local sheriffs. But that didn't stop him from going on the lam. While still serving on the nation's highest court, he was arrested and served time in debtors' prisons in New Jersey and North Carolina. His confinement was embarrassing for him, his second wife, Hannah Gray, his children, President John Adams, and the United States as a whole. He is not so much a forgotten founding father as one that many prefer to forget.

In 1798, probably after his release from one of those prisons, an on-the-run Wilson hid in a decrepit North Carolina tavern, where he was discovered by his wife, thirty years his junior and younger than some of his own grown children. Sick with malaria, he initially recovered but then suffered a stroke. Fellow justice James Iredell took pity on the couple and offered them shelter at his home in Edenton, North Carolina. (That house is now open to the public.) There, Wilson's mind finally snapped. He mumbled deliriously about arrest and bankruptcy before dying, close to his fifty-sixth birthday. He was buried at a nearby plantation. In 1906, his bones were moved just outside the walls of Christ Church in Philadelphia.

The Playboy with the Wooden Leg

BORN: January 31, 1752
DIED: November 6, 1816
AGE AT SIGNING: 35
PROFESSION: Lawyer, merchant
BURIED: St. Anne's Episcopal Churchyard, Bronx, New York

★ ★ ★ ★ ★ ★ ★ ★ ★ ★ ★ ★

If you can quote from memory just one line of the Constitution, chances are it's the famous opening written by Gouverneur Morris. A playboy with a gift for both gab and gallivanting, Morris was born at Morrisania, a spectacular estate named for his family (his mouthful of a moniker comes from his mother's maiden name) in what was then Westchester County, now the heart of the Bronx, New York. His family was one of the wealthiest and most influential in New York; his half-brother Lewis was a signer of the Declaration of Independence. Morris had every advantage, and then some: tutors when he was young, a stint at the Academy of Philadelphia (now the University of Pennsylvania, established by that city's patron saint, Ben Franklin), and a degree at King's College (now Columbia University). He was a great student, sure, but more notably he loved to write and had a way with words, whether spoken or written. The former of these gifts would earn him a reputation as someone whose tongue sometimes got away from him. The latter would give the Constitution its preamble, some of the most stirring language in the entire document.

Morris studied law in New York and then set up shop. Despite his money, connections, and some loyalist relatives to boot, Morris was a Whig, albeit a conservative one. He entered New York politics in 1775 and, in 1776, helped write that state's constitution, along with future chief justice John Jay and Robert R. Livingston. Throughout his life, Morris made speeches that were notable, if far from subtle: "Trust crocodiles, trust the hungry wolf in your flock, or a rattlesnake in your bosom—you may yet be something wise. But trust the King, his ministers, his commissioners—it is madness in the extreme!"

In a somewhat strange move for someone of his social and financial position, Morris took up with the New York militia. In 1777, he was a member of his city's Council of Safety, a wartime civilian watchdog group, and worked in the state legislature. He was a natural to attend the Continental Congress, and did so in 1778. He was immediately sent off to Valley Forge to check on how things were going with Washington and was gob-smacked at what he found there, describing to Congress the "naked, starving condition" of the army.

Morris did not mince words, whether on the floor of Congress or in the presence of ladies of a variety of reputations. But this talent did not always work to his advantage. In 1779, he was not reelected to Congress because of his disparaging comments about New York governor George Clinton, a known patriot and friend of Washington. Morris decided to remain in Philadelphia to work as a lawyer and merchant. He soon fell in with another wealthy and well-connected colleague who shared his surname—Robert Morris—signer of the Constitution and the Declaration of Independence.

The Morris–Morris friendship was a fruitful one. When Robert Morris was appointed the nation's superintendent of finance in 1781,

Signing Their Rights Away

he made Gouverneur his assistant, and the two worked together until 1785. Their alliance produced the charter for the country's first bank, the Bank of North America, a model upon which Alexander Hamilton likely based the first Bank of the United States. Gouverneur Morris suggested the decimal-based money system and offered the word *cent* in place of the oh-so-British term *penny* (although *penny* has hardly been eradicated from the modern American-English lexicon). But the nation found his system too complicated and switched to one suggested by Thomas Jefferson a few years later.

Morris's big moment came in 1787 at the Constitutional Convention, which he attended as part of the Pennsylvania delegation. That was where he shined. He was there at the very start but then was called away to New York for a month. Despite this absence, he made more speeches than any other delegate, a whopping 173. His presence was powerful and hard to miss. "Mr. Governeur Morris . . . winds through all the mazes of rhetoric, and throws around him such a glare that he charms, captivates, and leads away the senses of all who hear him," wrote Georgia delegate William Pierce. "With an infinite stretch of fancy he brings to view things when he is engaged in deep argumentation, that render all the labor of reasoning easy and pleasing. . . . This Gentleman . . . has been unfortunate in losing one of his Legs, and getting all the flesh taken off his right arm by a scald, when a youth."

The leg incident to which Pierce refers was the result of a carriage accident that injured Morris's leg. Nowadays, such an incident would result in a little surgery and eight weeks in a cast—but the founding fathers didn't have the luxury of modern medical technologies. Morris's accident occurred out of town and far from his fancy Philadelphia physician. The limb was removed and he was fitted with a wooden leg that the six-foot-tall Morris wore for the rest of his life. When he returned home to Philadelphia, his personal physician said the leg probably could have been saved. Regardless, the injury apparently did not dampen his extracurricular activities. A popular rumor held that Morris—a bachelor with a reputation for being a bit of playboy—had in fact lost his leg while leaping from a window to escape an angry husband who caught Morris attempting "a great compromise" with the man's wife.

At the convention, Morris was among the large-state nationalists favoring the Virginia Plan, and he believed that taxes should be paid in proportion to a state's population (that is, the bigger the population, the higher the taxes the state should pay). He did not want the president to be chosen by Congress, but rather by citizens. (Yet, to this day, the Electoral College remains one of the most contested and, for many, annoyingly outdated, vestigial organs of the Constitutional Convention.)

Morris was also one of the most frequent and forceful—if not *the* most forceful—voices against slavery, referring to it as "the curse of heaven on the States where it prevailed." In addition, he proposed the idea of a presidential cabinet, calling it the "Council of State," and served on a couple committees. While John Rutledge and the rest of the Committee of Detail were working to roll all the ideas proposed at the convention into some sort of workable first draft, the other delegates took a break. Morris traveled with George Washington and others to Valley Forge, where they reminisced about the old days and fished for trout.

So on September 8, 1787, as everyone was hoping to wrap up the convention, they took a look at the draft created by Rutledge's team. The content got a pass, but it was agreed that the prose was lacking. Enter the Committee of Style and Arrangement, charged with polishing the draft. The chairman of this committee was Connecticut's William Samuel Johnson, whose team included Alexander Hamilton, James Madison, Rufus King, and Morris. Many claimed that Morris was to the Committee of Style what Jefferson was to the Committee of Five, which drew up the Declaration of Independence; as Madison himself later wrote, "The finish given to the style and arrangement of the Constitution, fairly belongs to the pen of Mr. Morris."

His pen gave the United States the beautiful, most oft-quoted words of the Constitution, the Preamble: *"We the people of the United States, in Order to form a more perfect Union, establish Justice, insure domestic Tranquility, provide for the common defence, promote the general Welfare, and secure the Blessings of Liberty to ourselves and our Posterity, do ordain and establish this Constitution for the United States of America."*

Upon completion, the stylized version was presented to the convention, edits were made, and an engrossed copy (read: fancy paper, fancy penmanship) of the Constitution was ordered from Jacob Shallus, a clerk working in the State House (see "The Penman of the Constitution," page 237).

On September 17, the chips were down. Franklin called for unanimous acceptance of the completed document. Virginia governor Edmund Randolph, who had stayed to the bitter end of the convention, said he couldn't do it—there was no way nine states would ratify what the men had created, and he left without signing. According to Madison's notes, Morris responded that, sure, the document wasn't perfect, but it was "the best that could be attained." He later wrote to John Dickinson: "In adopting a republican form of government, I not only took it as a man does his wife, for better or worse, but what few men do with their wives: I took it knowing all its bad qualities." The time had come to decide whether there would be a national government. If not, chaos would reign. "The moment this plan goes forth all other considerations will be laid aside—and the great question will be, shall there be a national Government or not?"

After ratification, Morris traveled to France and England. In 1792, Washington officially appointed him the U.S. Minister, or ambassador, to France, replacing Thomas Jefferson. While in that country, Morris witnessed the French Revolution, which he described in his diaries and letters. Morris was replaced in 1794 by James Monroe, but he stayed in Europe for travel, business, and, hey, let's be frank—probably the company of some lovely French ladies. His diary entries from that period are at once salacious and sublime.

He recounts steamy encounters with numerous women—married and single, old and young, sisters—in passageways, carriages, even a Parisian convent. Some of the entries read like a modern-day bodice-ripper: "She had the remains of a fine form and a countenance open and expressive . . . but they were wearing fast away. Neither had nature quite lost her empire, for the tints, which love in retiring to the heart had shed over her countenance, were slightly tinged with desire. I thought I could, in a single look, read half her history." Ooh-la-la! Morris even set his sights on Dolley Madison (wife of fellow signer James Madison) and at one point writes in his diary of seeing her in a low-cut dress and wondering if she is "amenable to seduction."

When Morris returned to the United States, he moved into Morrisania, his family's vast estate. He was a senator for the state of New York in 1800, serving until 1803. A staunch Federalist, he campaigned in favor of John Adams and against Thomas Jefferson in the testy election of 1800. He feared mob rule and thought government posts should be reserved for those with money and family clout.

As he aged, Morris suffered from gout and other ailments, but the peg-legged playboy still had a few tricks up his sleeves. On Christmas Day 1809, he shocked his family and friends by announcing that he was getting married—and then called in a preacher and his fiancée and got hitched on the spot! His bride was Anne "Nancy" Cary Randolph, a woman with a checkered past from a prominent Virginia family. At age eighteen, she had given birth to the baby of her brother-in-law Richard, who was later charged with murdering the child. The great patriot Patrick Henry defended the pair, and they were acquitted. But the scandal ruined Anne's reputation as well as her chances of landing a husband, and so she fled north, where she eventually ended up working as a housekeeper in Morris's house. Their marriage was apparently a happy one. They had a son, who was burdened with his father's name—Gouverneur II—but was bolstered by his father's wealth. Morris had become a dad at sixty-one.

Signing Their Rights Away

In the last years of his life, Morris worked on the Erie Canal and became president of the New-York Historical Society. (His wooden leg is on display there, in the same case as President Franklin Delano Roosevelt's polio brace.) Just three years after the birth of his son, Morris died at Morrisania in the same room in which he was born. His grave can be visited today, an underground vault under an oasis of green in the urban sprawl of the Bronx.

★ ★ ★ ★ ★ ★ ★ ★ ★ ★ ★ ★

VII. Delaware

Geo. Read

★ ★ ★ ★ ★ ★ ★ ★ ★ ★ ★ ★

The Signer Who Signed Twice

BORN: September 18, 1733
DIED: September 21, 1798
AGE AT SIGNING: 53
PROFESSION: Lawyer
BURIED: Immanuel Episcopal
    Churchyard, New Castle,
    Delaware

★ ★ ★ ★ ★ ★ ★ ★ ★ ★ ★ ★

George Read is one of only six men who signed both the Declaration of Independence and the Constitution—and, on both occasions, he was something of an exception. When he put his pen to the Declaration, he was the only signer who had voted *against* independence on July 2, 1776. And when he signed the Constitution, he did so twice—the first time for himself, and the second for a friend.

Born in Maryland, Read and his family moved to Delaware when he was a child. He later journeyed to nearby Philadelphia to study law in the office of John Moland, the same office in which his friend and fellow signer John Dickinson learned his trade. Eventually Read knew enough to set out on his own, and he opened his own practice in New Castle, Delaware. There he married Gertrude Ross Till, the widowed sister of soon-to-be fellow Declaration signer George Ross, and the couple got to work making their family of five children. Read was a stand-up guy, by all accounts, and in 1763 was working for the Crown as attorney general of the Three Lower Counties, as Delaware was then known. But in 1765, his role in public life changed. That was the year of the Stamp Tax, the notorious British levy on all paper documents and products, which Read protested. He resigned his post as attorney general and became a member of the Delaware legislature.

When Read attended the first and second Continental Congresses, he wasn't your typical tar-and-feather patriot. Yes, he was against the taxes the British kept lobbing across the pond. And yes, he was all for punitively reducing British goods. He even raised money to help Boston citizens when they were reeling from the closing of their port (punishment for the famous Tea Party). But like his friend and fellow signer John Dickinson, Read desired neither war nor independence—at least not yet. On the contrary, Read hoped that the colonies and Mother England would find some way to kiss and make up.

Alas, that was not to be. But Read, a principled kind of guy, voted his conscience on July 2, 1776. And his conscience said *no*—the colonies should not break with Britain. It was a unique position: there were plenty of waffling congressmen who abstained from the vote or who abstained and later signed it. Read was alone in that he voted "no" and then proceeded to sign the treasonous Declaration of Independence anyway. (Years later, Read's grandson wrote a book attempting to explain his grandpa's motivation. Simply put, Read thought that taking on the Crown was too risky; Britain was a world superpower, and the colonies barely had enough money to buy ammunition for their small, inexperienced military. Hard to argue with that.)

But the majority had spoken, and Read respected their wishes—he signed the Declaration along with the rest of them. Pennsylvania delegate Joseph Galloway said Read did so "with a rope about his neck." Read quipped, "I know the risk, and am prepared for all consequences."

He supported the war effort wholeheartedly. Back in Delaware, he chaired the committee to draft the Delaware Constitution and was also vice president (assistant governor) of the state. Along the way, he experienced an up-close-and-personal scare at the hands of the enemy. When Governor John McKinly was captured by the British, assistant governor Read was called to take over. While heading south from Philadelphia with his family, Read attempted to cross the Delaware River, but their small boat ran aground in sight of a British ship. When the Redcoats descended, quick-thinking Read told them he was just a local guy taking his wife and kids home. The soldiers believed the ruse and even helped the treasonous colonial governor to shore.

Read served until 1778, and shortly after his health began to decline. He resigned from his public activities for a spell but returned in 1782 as a judge of the court of appeals in admiralty cases. When the Annapolis Convention came around, Read was there. He didn't want the Articles of Confederation to be altered; he wanted them scrapped, period. Anything less, Madison quoted him as saying, "would be like putting new cloth on an old garment."

Read brought this same passion to the Constitutional Convention, where he was a major force for the rights of small states. Since Rhode Island played hooky at the gathering, Read and the other Delaware delegates were representing the smallest state. Although he was a straightforward man who believed in speaking his mind, he was not exactly celebrated for his off-the-cuff speaking skills. Still, anyone who underestimated Read didn't do so for long. He was a respected delegate, one of the few who had also signed the Declaration of Independence, and his distrust of large states had been brewing for a long time. He'd had a hand in shaping Delaware's instructions for the convention delegates, which included a mandate not to give up the "one state, one vote" right that had been in the Articles of Confederation. So when Madison proposed, and

Signing Their Rights Away

Gouverneur Morris seconded, the idea of representation based on population, Read told them to table the conversation or Delaware would "retire from the Convention." It was only May 30, just two weeks into the proceedings, and already a small state was threatening to hit the road. Read's wishes were respected, and the representation discussion was postponed.

Read said he favored the United States "doing away with the states altogether, and uniting them all into one society." So, like New Jersey's David Brearley, he was ready to erase boundaries and redraw the national map. Read had equally strong feelings about paper money and was vehemently opposed to giving Congress the power to "emit bills," or print paper money. Read said those words had to go, and, if they did not, it "would be as alarming as the mark of the Beast in Revelations." His point: paper money was intrinsically worthless. Why should one man's paper money be valued the same as another man's gold? The line was removed.

When all was said and done, Delaware supported the Great Compromise, which gave small states equal representation in the Senate. And so Read went on to sign—the first to do so for what would become the so-called First State—and then some. When his old pal John Dickinson, a Quaker lawyer and gentleman farmer, was forced by illness to leave before the signing ceremony, he instructed Read to sign in his place. That made Read the only delegate to sign the Constitution twice. Delaware went on to become the first state to ratify.

Read served as one of his state's first two senators in the new government he played such a significant part in framing. He was a staunch Federalist and supporter of Alexander Hamilton's national finance system. He left Congress in 1793 and served as chief justice of Delaware's supreme court. Read died in New Castle at age sixty-five, his life and efforts having helped little Delaware earn the big rep as the very first state.

The Signer Who Trusted No One

BORN: 1747
DIED: Marh 30, 1812
AGE AT SIGNING: About 40
PROFESSION: Lawyer, judge
BURIED: Masonic Home
    Cemetery, Christiana,
    Delaware

★ ★ ★ ★ ★ ★ ★ ★ ★ ★ ★ ★

Gunning Bedford Jr.'s story is filled with mysterious gaps. No one knows his birthday. His early years are a blur. And details of his military record—if indeed he even served in the Revolutionary War—are so spotty that military biographers tend to omit him entirely from their catalog of soldier-signers. Luckily for us, however, he springs most vividly to life in the history of the Constitutional Convention, where his rants crystallized the deepest fears of all the delegates.

This oversized, tempestuous delegate was born in Philadelphia, the son of an architect. Young Gunning didn't enter college until he was twenty, which made him the old man on campus in Princeton, New Jersey. One of his roomies was James Madison, the future president and father of the U.S. Constitution. By the time he graduated, the affable, sociable Gunning had acquired a wife, Jane Ballaroux

Parker, who brought the couple's first child to hear Bedford's valedictorian speech in 1771.

Bedford studied law in Philadelphia but moved to Dover, Delaware, to practice in 1779; eventually the family moved to a townhouse in Wilmington. No one has ever found records of Bedford's service during the Revolutionary War, but his daughter described him in her will as an aide-de-camp to Washington; she bequeathed to the Smithsonian a pair of pistols, which she said the good general had given her father as protection during a secret mission from Trenton to New York. After the war, Bedford was elected to the Continental Congress and, shortly after, began working as attorney general for Delaware.

By the time he showed up in Philadelphia for the Constitutional Convention, Bedford was all too aware of the current government's deficiencies. And since Rhode Island had refused to send delegates to the convention, he and his fellow Delawareans were representing the single smallest state. Bedford spoke often and had a penchant for making impolitic statements; historians have described him as impulsive, impetuous, rash, agitated, and quick to temper.

In one early-June session, he erupted, accusing the big states of "crushing" the others or having a "monstrous influence" on matters. On the last day of the month, a sweltering Saturday, when the small states had presented their compromise, the big-state delegates still clung stubbornly to an all-or-nothing position: the Senate must also be based on a proportion of the population. Bedford leapt to his feet and denounced the big states, saving his sternest condemnation for the three southernmost states, the Carolinas and Georgia, which didn't have huge populations but were nevertheless siding with the big states in anticipation that one day they, too, would be big. His double chins flapping in the heat, Bedford then railed at all the big states in general: *"I do not, gentlemen, trust you!* If you possess the power, the abuse of it could not be checked.... The small states can never agree to the Virginia Plan ... Is it come to this, then, that the sword must decide this controversy? Will you crush the small states, must they be left unmolested? Sooner than be ruined, *there are for-eign powers who will take us by the hand!*"

With these words, Bedford had summarized the profound un-derlying fear of the convention: the attendees were terrified of being dominated and controlled by their fellow states. Working together they had shucked off a monarch. Who in their right mind would now voluntarily sign away their rights to Massachusetts, Pennsylva-nia, or Virginia? Bedford's reference to the sword was an all-too-prescient suggestion of all-out civil war. But his veiled threat that the small states would ally themselves with foreign powers was as childishly irrational as it was unlikely. And yet, his words echoed in the delegates' minds when they adjourned for Sunday. Upon return-ing for a vote on Monday, Georgia sided with the small states, and for the first time the entire delegation realized that in order to save the union the small states had to get their way on *something*. They were far from finished, but the logjam had been broken.

The other delegates asked Bedford to sit on the committee that hammered out the details of the Great Compromise. Either they respected his opinions or they hoped to buy his silence by allowing him to have input on this critical matter. Once the idea of a bicam-eral legislature was set in stone, Bedford fought off any attempts to limit its power. "Mr. Bedford was opposed to every check on the Legislative," James Madison wrote at one point, practically sighing with exhaustion over his quill. Bedford signed the Constitution and went home to promote it at his state's ratifying convention.

Bedford was passed over for the House and Senate in the new Congress but was picked by George Washington to be the first U.S. district judge for Delaware, a bench he occupied till the end of his days. He and his wife bought a 250-acre farm outside Wilmington, where they derived a nice income from crops and enjoyed some town and country socializing. He was active in education, served as the first president of Wilmington College, and became an aboli-tionist. Never regarded as a brilliant or profound jurist, the convention's corpulent hothead mellowed into an able judge of moderate talents. He died in the spring of 1812, when he was sixty-five years old. He was buried in a Presbyterian churchyard, but his body was later moved to a Masonic cemetery, where he is a prominent resident. The bullet-shaped monument over his grave hints at his size, proclaiming, "His form was goodly."

★ ★ ★ ★ ★ ★ ★ ★ ★ ★ ★ ★

John Dickinson

****

The Signer Who Never Signed

BORN: November 8, 1732
DIED: February 14, 1808
AGE AT SIGNING: 54
PROFESSION: Lawyer
BURIED: Friends Burial Ground,
Wilmington, Delaware

****

He supported the revolutionary cause but was opposed to the Declaration of Independence. He sought a peaceful resolution to the colonies' troubles with Britain yet joined the militia. He hailed from teeny-tiny Delaware but supported nationalist policies that favored his larger neighbors. At first blush, John Dickinson appears to be all over the map on issues of independence and government—but the reality is much simpler: throughout his life, Dickinson was true to his ideals and his countrymen, and he was always willing to do what was asked by his country, including compromise.

Born in Maryland to a fairly wealthy landowner, Dickinson was raised in a Quaker family; his father was a judge. Young John grew up on an estate, surrounded by books and educated by tutors. After clerking in a law office, he studied law at Middle Temple in London, a popular choice for well-educated men of the day (and the alma mater of more than a few signers of the Declaration of Independence and the Constitution).

Returning colony-side in 1757, he practiced law in Philadelphia. Having a foothold in both Delaware and Pennsylvania gave Dickinson some interesting political options. At the time, the two states had separate legislatures but shared a governor. Dickinson began his political career in Delaware but over the years would serve in both colonies' legislatures. The Stamp Act of 1765, the infamous tax on paper documents, set Dickinson's pen in motion, and the ink kept flowing for the rest of his life. He represented Pennsylvania at the 1765 Stamp Act Congress in New York, where he wrote the "Declaration of Rights and Grievances," which stated that "no taxes be imposed on them but with their own consent, given personally, or by their representatives." The Congress was considered a success, and the tax was (temporarily) repealed. Dickinson believed that the colonists should have the same rights as British subjects living across the pond. He was already on his way to earning a nickname that would stay with him throughout his life: the Penman of the Revolution.

Beginning in 1767, Britain introduced the Townshend Acts, which brought higher taxes for daily staples such as paint, paper, and the colonists' beloved tea. In response, Dickinson penned a famed series of essays, "Letters from a Farmer in Pennsylvania to the Inhabitants of the British Colonies." A hard-working lawyer and farmer himself, Dickinson spoke out against unfair taxation but stopped short of encouraging an uprising: "Be upon your guard against those, who may at any time endeavour to stir you up, under pretences of patriotism, to any measures disrespectful to our Sovereign and our mother country . . ."

In 1770, Dickinson married Mary Norris, the only child of one of Philadelphia's richest men, and the couple moved to a large estate. Moderate, nonviolent Dickinson was a delegate to the first Continental Congress, in 1774, and sparred with the more radical or "violent" New England faction. Dickinson favored boycotts of British goods—hit them in their coin purse, he said. He wrote a "Petition to the King" that was later adopted by Congress. "We ask but for peace, liberty, and safety," he wrote. But John Adams and other hardliners read his words as a softball; they wanted more. Dickinson didn't care: "If you don't concur with us in our pacific system, I and a number of us will break off from you in New England, and we will carry on the opposition by ourselves in our own way."

The stakes were higher at the second Continental Congress, in 1775. Skirmishes between British troops and colonists were heating up, and Dickinson introduced his "Declaration on the Causes and Necessity of Taking Up Arms" (along with coauthor Thomas Jefferson). "Our cause is just," it stated. "Our union is perfect." These statements sound bold until you read the words that soon follow them: "We mean not to dissolve that union which has so long and so happily subsisted between us, and which we sincerely wish to see restored."

Dickinson was opposed to Richard Henry Lee's famed resolution on June 7, 1776, which called for the colonies to break with Britain. He thought the timing simply wasn't right, that the colonies could resolve the situation without a war. The "Olive Branch Petition" was Dickinson's last stab at making nice with George III, but the impetus toward independence had already left the gate. Rather than vote for or against independence, Dickinson stayed home when the vote was taken on July 2, 1776. By abstaining, he allowed Pennsylvania to vote yea, and the rest is hot dog and fireworks history. He differed greatly from his buddy Robert Morris, who also abstained. Morris went on to sign the Declaration of Independence, but Dickinson would not. He was not reelected to Congress at the time but did his best to support the majority. He joined the militia, starting out as a private and finishing as a brigadier general, ending his soldier days in 1777.

While Jefferson toiled on the Declaration, Dickinson and a small committee crafted guidelines for this new independent nation. He became the primary author of the Articles of Confederation. In

1779, Dickinson signed his document when he returned to Congress, this time as a Delaware delegate. He went back to colonial politics in 1780, serving on the Delaware Assembly, and in 1781 was elected president (as chief execs of colonies were often called) of Delaware. He stayed in that post until 1782, when he became president of Pennsylvania. The jobs overlapped by a couple months, so Dickinson was governor of both states simultaneously.

Not one to view his writing as too precious to touch, Dickinson agreed that the Articles of Confederation needed revision. He chaired the Annapolis Convention of 1786, the precursor to the Constitutional Convention. A year later, at the 1787 convention, Dickinson cut an interesting figure and was often described as sickly, emaciated, and habitually clad in black. He brought to mind an underfed Puritan, though he was in fact a very well fed Quaker. Though he favored a strong central government, he was still a vocal advocate for the small states, stating, "Rule by a foreign power would be preferable to domination by large states."

In the end, Dickinson—who was sick during much of the convention—could not attend the signing ceremony on September 17, 1787. George Read, his fellow Delaware delegate and friend, signed for him, making Dickinson the only signer of the Constitution who did not physically sign the document for himself. Once ratification was under way, however, Dickinson, writing under the pen name "Fabius," encouraged citizens to support the new Constitution. His efforts helped Delaware become the first state.

After retiring at age sixty, Dickinson wrote additional letters as Fabius, criticizing John Adams's administration. He founded Dickinson College in Carlisle, Pennsylvania, contributing books and about seven hundred acres to the school. His life ended at home at age seventy-five, a loss noted by Thomas Jefferson: "A more estimable man or truer patriot could not have left us . . . his name will be consecrated in history as one of the great worthies of the revolution." Dickinson's house and plantation, Poplar Hall, are open to the public today.

Richard Bassett

★ ★ ★ ★ ★ ★ ★ ★ ★ ★ ★ ★ ★

The Signer Who Overcame Religious Discrimination

BORN: April 2, 1745

DIED: August 16 or
September 15, 1815

AGE AT SIGNING: 54

PROFESSION: Lawyer, planter

BURIED: Wilmington and
Brandywine Cemetery,
Wilmington, Delaware

★ ★ ★ ★ ★ ★ ★ ★ ★ ★ ★ ★

George W. Bush was one. So was his vice president, Dick Cheney. Hilary Clinton was one, and they still let her serve. Today, Methodists make up the third-largest religious denomination in the United States. But during the Founding era, this offshoot of Anglicanism was still in its missionary stage, and its adherents were looked upon with suspicion by American patriots. None of the signers of the Declaration of Independence were Methodists, and only two Constitution signers were members of that denomination.

Richard Bassett, one of those two men, was born in the northeastern corner of Maryland, just under the site of the present Pennsylvania border. When his tavern-keeper father, Arnold, ran out on the family, Richard's mother, Judith, allowed her son to be raised by her wealthy relative Peter Lawson, who trained Bassett in the law and later bequeathed to him Bohemia Manor, a massive, six-thousand-acre estate near the Delaware border. He would spend the rest of his life split between the two states.

Bassett practiced law in Dover and later Wilmington, Delaware. At first reluctant to bear arms against his king, he eventually served as a rebel captain of a Dover troop of light-horse militia. During the war, he met one of the nation's first Methodist bishops, the charismatic Francis Asbury, and became a convert in 1779 (at a time when it was generally assumed that all Methodists were Tories). One night while the war raged, a mob appeared at the door of Bassett's home while a local Methodist judge was dining inside. They demanded that Bassett hand over the man for punishment. The normally cheerful, affectionate Bassett donned his militia gear and went to the door brandishing his pistol and waving his sword. He defended his friend, saying he was no Tory. *If you thugs want to manhandle the judge*, Bassett said, *you have to kill me first!* The overzealous patriot mob melted away.

The signer's military service was brief, for he resigned from full-time active duty upon being sent to the Delaware legislature in 1776. He served in the legislature for a decade, right up to the year the Constitutional Convention was called. Bassett had attended the Annapolis Convention in 1786 and believed, as many did, that the government needed to remake itself or risk falling apart. By the time Bassett arrived in Philadelphia for the convention, his reputation had preceded him. He was one of the wealthiest participants, with two homes and another vast plantation. He had lobbied hard (and failed) to end the practice of slavery in his state. He had also funded a Methodist church in Dover and delivered sermons as a Methodist lay preacher.

Bassett lodged in Philadelphia at a tavern that was a home away from home to several delegates, including John Rutledge and Charles Pinckney of South Carolina; Dr. Hugh Williamson, the star-gazing physician from North Carolina; Nathaniel Gorham of Massachusetts;

and the brilliant but difficult Alexander Hamilton of New York. Nestled in their cozy quarters, these men from different walks of life and states of the union could socialize, raise a few pints, and discuss the affairs of the day. In this environment, they could view one another as real men, flesh-and-blood comrades, and not as overbearing self-interested politicians. Such a convivial situation went a long way toward softening Bassett's position on the big vs. small state debates. He didn't contribute much to the debates and served on no committees, but he never missed a session. He probably supported the New Jersey Plan and voted often with Dickinson and Read in favor of a strong central government. He signed the Constitution at the end of the summer and went home to pitch the new document to his fellow future first-staters.

Soon afterward, Bassett was elected one of the first two Delaware senators to serve in the country's new Congress. In that role, he was instrumental in designing the structure of the American court system. In favor of moving the nation's capital from New York City to a more politically neutral territory, he voted for the creation of the District of Columbia. When he left Congress in 1793, he focused on state politics for the rest of his life, first as a judge and later as Delaware's governor. A lifelong Federalist, he was one of the "midnight judges" John Adams tried to appoint during the waning hours of his presidency, under a statute of the Judiciary Act of 1801 (which Adams had hastily passed before leaving office). But before Bassett could ascend to the bench, newly minted president Thomas Jefferson blocked the appointments—a move that was later supported by the Supreme Court in the famous case *Marbury v. Madison*, which found that Adams's Judiciary Act was unconstitutional.

In his later years, Bassett lived happily on his vast estate. He hosted Methodist camp meetings, entertained countless guests, and indulged a passion for philanthropy. But a series of strokes left him increasingly weak and helpless. He died in 1815, at the age of seventy, although this signer's descendants served in Congress well into the twentieth century.

Jacob Broom [signature]

The Invisible Signer

BORN: 1752

DIED: April 25, 1810

AGE AT SIGNING: About 35

PROFESSION: Surveyor, farmer, businessman

BURIED: Christ Church, Philadelphia, Pennsylvania

★ ★ ★ ★ ★ ★ ★ ★ ★ ★ ★ ★

acob Broom is so obscure . . .

How obscure is he?

He's so obscure, we're not even sure what he looks like. Good luck trying to find him in Howard Chandler Christy's famous 1940 mural *Scene at the Signing of the Constitution of the United States*; in that painting, Broom's face is blocked by the head of fellow signer John Dickinson. Other books on the signers show Broom's face in dark silhouette or merely replaced by an artful question mark. A verified image of him has never been found, and so he's the only signer whose looks are a mystery.

Luckily, what Broom accomplished is not in question, though

history hasn't always done justice to this small-state signer with a big heart. He may not have spoken often, but in one memorable moment he prevented the entire convention from shutting down. Without his bold actions, the Constitution might not exist.

Broom was born in Wilmington, Delaware, the only Constitution signer to be born in the First State. Believed to be descended from the royal Plantagenet family in England—Plantagenet means "broom-plant"—Broom was the son of a blacksmith-turned-farmer and a Quaker mother. Though not tremendously wealthy, the family did have land holdings, silver, and gold; they were solidly gentry. Broom was schooled at home and at the Wilmington Old Academy. He studied surveying and became a merchant and land dealer. He married Rachel Pierce in 1773, and the couple had eight children.

Broom was less active in politics than many of his cosigners, but he was a successful businessman and dabbled in the local politics of Wilmington, his hometown. He was a justice of the peace (which, at the time, didn't require a law degree) and a borough assessor. He was also an assistant burgess, an elected representative of the people six times over, and went on to be chief burgess, a post he held four times.

Broom put his surveying talents to use for General George Washington, drawing maps used during the 1777 battle of Brandywine Creek in Pennsylvania. The two men developed an appreciation for each other. After the American Revolution ended in victory, Washington arrived in Wilmington to a hero's reception—there was a thirteen-gun salute, an extravagant meal, and an impassioned speech from Broom: "Your glorious endeavors to rescue our country from a determined plan of oppression have been not only attended with the most brilliant success, but crowned with the noble rewards of liberty, independence, and the final accomplishment of an honorable peace." He also encouraged Washington, "that with a parental consideration, your excellency will occasionally contribute your advice and influence to promote the harmony and union of our infant governments which are so essential to the permanent establishment of our freedom, happiness, and prosperity."

Broom's brief stint in state and national office began in 1784, when he was elected to the Delaware legislature. He served three terms. He was chosen to go to the Annapolis Convention but did not attend. However, he was present for the opening session of the Constitutional Convention, on May 25, 1787, and voted to elect Washington as convention president.

Broom was not especially talkative during the debates. He reportedly suggested Wilmington as the future capital of the United States, an idea that went nowhere. He seconded fellow Delaware delegate George Read's motion for nine-year senate terms and believed national legislators should be paid by Congress. He supported the idea that a president should be chosen by electors appointed by the state legislature, rather than by the people themselves, and he felt the president should serve for life, as long as he behaved himself. He was not afraid of giving power to a strong national government and agreed with South Carolinian Charles Pinckney that Congress should have the power to veto legislation passed by a state, if it saw fit.

On those few occasions when Broom did speak up, his words were delivered with plenty of conviction. As a representative of the smallest state, he agreed that if representation in the House was going to be based on population, then everyone should have an equal voice in the Senate. This, he said to his fellow delegates, "could not be denied after this concession of the small States as to the first branch."

By July 16, the battle over representation in Congress was coming to a head. Talk of an adjournment *sine die*—meaning indefinitely—appeared likely. Everyone feared that an indefinite adjournment would mean the delegates would leave the talks and never return.

But then, out of the thick and steamy Philadelphia summer heat, rose the usually quiet Jacob Broom. *Sine die* was not an option. It would be disastrous. He pleaded with his fellow delegates that "something must be done by the Convention, though it should be by a bare majority."

Jaws dropped. *Who was this little broom-plant to speak so passionately?*

But somehow the plea worked. Congress agreed to adjourn not

indefinitely, but only until the next day, at which point they would continue to hammer out the details. The convention—and the Constitution—was saved. If news of his valiant effort had been circulated more widely among local artists, perhaps we'd have a portrait of Broom today. Alas, no such luck.

Broom returned to local politics and was active in Wilmington for the remainder of his years. He helped found the town's first library in 1787. Washington appointed him first postmaster of Wilmington in 1790, and he worked as head of the water, sewer, and street departments. He was a seventeen-year trustee in the Wilmington Academy, which became the College of Wilmington. He was a lay leader active in the Old Swedes Church and served as director of the board of the Bank of Delaware and the Wilmington Bridge Company, which constructed, among other things, a toll bridge. If only Broom could see tiny Delaware now! How he would marvel at the four American dollars required to travel from Wilmington to the Maryland state line—a distance of a mere thirty miles.

And Broom still found time for his business pursuits. In 1795, he opened the first cotton mill in that part of the country and, two years later, built an even larger one along the Brandywine River, which later burned down. It took several years before he rebuilt it, and he eventually sold the land, which was equipped with a dam and a millrace, to Eleuthère Irénée du Pont. The property became a part of the massive du Pont empire. Today, the area is a national historic site in Wilmington, and visitors may tour Hagley Museum and Library, which celebrates American industrial history and enterprise from the eighteenth century to the present. Jacob Broom's house is located nearby, not far from the original cotton mill. It is a private residence.

Broom died at age fifty-eight in Philadelphia and is buried in Christ Church Burial Ground. Yet even posthumously he continued his contributions to society; he left money to the Female Benevolent Society, which served women in need, and the Wilmington Association for Promoting the Education of People of Color, a school established to educate black children.

VIII. Maryland

James McHenry [signature]

The Signer Immortalized by the Star-Spangled Banner

BORN: November 16, 1753
DIED: May 3, 1816
AGE AT SIGNING: 33
PROFESSION: Merchant, doctor
BURIED: Westminster Hall
    Burying Ground, Baltimore,
    Maryland

Many Americans know the story of the Star-Spangled Banner, the flag that flew high over Fort McHenry, in the Chesapeake Bay, during the War of 1812. The bombs burst, the rockets glared, and in the end the flag was still there. Although it's a powerful tale, few people can identify the namesake of that famous fort. He is James McHenry, an Irish immigrant signer of the Constitution who reached the upper echelons of the new American government—only to be booted out of office by a jealous and paranoid president.

McHenry was born in what is now Northern Ireland. In 1771, his wealthy merchant parents sent him to America, where he studied medicine with Benjamin Rush, the famous physician and signer of the Declaration of Independence. McHenry's flowery descriptions of his new homeland persuaded his parents to send his brother to the colonies as well. Later, the whole family joined them and opened a prosperous store in Baltimore. While in his early twenties, McHenry took part in the fighting during the Revolutionary War, serving as an army sawbones. He was captured by the British in New York, ministered to American troops while in confinement, and was later released on parole; he was allowed to return home to his parents' store under the condition that he take no further action on the American side. He obeyed this regulation until 1778, when he was "freed" in a prisoner exchange. He immediately went back to war, ministering to troops at Valley Forge and performing the duties of an aide-de-camp under Washington and the Marquis de Lafayette. During this time he became bosom buddies with Alexander Hamilton, who led troops under Lafayette's command.

Chosen by Maryland to serve in the state legislature, McHenry waited until the British surrendered at Yorktown before resigning his post and heading to Annapolis. He served there and in Congress for a few years. He also gave up medicine forever, thanks to a healthy inheritance from his father, who died in 1782. Now financially independent, McHenry took up poetry and sent his work to friends and loved ones, including a woman named Peggy Caldwell, whom he married in 1784.

Sent by his state to the Constitutional Convention, McHenry intended to be present for all the sessions, but in fact he was absent between June 1 and August 4 to tend to his sick brother in Baltimore. When he was in attendance at the debates, he took copious personal notes, which have provided historians with insight into the process and worldview of this earnest but lightweight politician. In his own notes William Pierce, the Georgia delegate, took jabs at McHenry: "He is a Man of specious [talents], with nothing of genius to improve them. As a politician there is nothing remarkable in him, nor has he any of the graces of the Orator."

Now, admittedly, McHenry tried to sit on the fence during the debates, which was problematic because the five delegates from

Maryland

Maryland were often split philosophically. (Only three would ultimately sign the document.) When McHenry was in attendance and voting, he was usually able to throw this swing state into the nationalist—that is, big government—camp. After signing the Constitution in September, McHenry tried to justify his actions in his journal, in which he comes off like a bewildered, nervous little man who knows he's out of his league. "I distrust my own judgment," he confessed, "especially as it is opposite to the opinion of a majority of gentlemen whose abilities and patriotism are of first cast; and as I have already frequent occasions to be convinced that I have not always judged right." Determined to give the Constitution the push it needed, he returned to Maryland and persuaded his fellow citizens to accept it. They did, and Maryland became the seventh state to ratify.

McHenry worked another eight years in state politics and no doubt would have lapsed into obscurity if not for his old commander, George Washington. Now president for a second term, Washington was casting about for a secretary of war. Three men turned him down before he hit upon asking his old administrative officer, McHenry. The Baltimore sawbones-turned-shopkeeper-turned-statesman took the job in 1796. He presided over many important new tasks, including, among others, enlarging the army and navy under the new Constitution, ordering construction of warships, and raising money to construct the star-shaped fort in Baltimore's port that would be named in his honor.

But McHenry often seemed to be floundering under a morass of paperwork. He relied on his old friend Hamilton for advice and sometimes parroted Hamilton's ideas directly in reports. His leadership was so incompetent that eventually even Hamilton—who never shied away from giving offense—complained to Washington: "My friend McHenry is wholly inefficient for his place, with the additional misfortune of not having the least suspicion of the fact." The old general's response must have shocked Hamilton: "I early discovered, after he entered upon the duties of his office, that his talents were unequal to great exertions, or deep resources. In truth, they were not expected, for the fact is, it was a Hobson's choice."

The stilted language of the eighteenth century might blunt the impact of this statement, so allow us to paraphrase: the man running the defense of these young United States, hand-picked by George Washington, was, by the general's own admission, an inept Hobson's choice, or a free choice in which only one option is offered.

Of course, then as now, political posts were sometimes rewards for loyalty, and Washington did display a tendency to repay his friends and former aides with high-paying jobs—but this kind of cronyism seems extreme. Incredibly, McHenry continued to serve in the same position under the next president, John Adams (most likely because there was no precedent for changing cabinets; Adams may have disliked Washington's staff, but he was stuck with them).

But when Adams lost the election of 1800 to Thomas Jefferson, the chief executive summoned McHenry to his office and asked for his resignation. McHenry was bowled over by the verbal insults; he would later write that Adams often spoke as if he were "actually insane." His dismissal is usually portrayed as unjustified, but some historians argue that McHenry truly was disloyal to Adams and had worked to sabotage his campaign.

No matter. McHenry had his life—and his writing—to return to. Now forty-six, he slunk back into private life at his country estate outside Baltimore, wrote poetry, socialized with friends, worked for his local Bible society, and in general stayed out of the limelight. Despite his association with the War of 1812, he bitterly opposed it, as did most Federalists. In a remarkable coincidence, his son fought at Fort McHenry during the same battle at which the national anthem was written. In the last years of his life, McHenry was struck with paralysis and could no longer walk. He died in 1816, at age sixty-two, and is buried in the same cemetery as Edgar Allan Poe.

* * * * * * * * * * * *

The Signer with the Mysterious Middle Name

BORN: 1723
DIED: November 16, 1790
AGE AT SIGNING: About 64
PROFESSION: Landowner, administrator
BURIED: Location unknown; somewhere near Port Tobacco, Maryland

★ ★ ★ ★ ★ ★ ★ ★ ★ ★ ★ ★

In an era before driver's licenses and social security numbers, the only way for people to establish their identity was to use their name and the place in which they were born or lived. For example, when one wealthy signer of the Declaration of Independence put his pen to that document, he used his name and the name of his estate: "Charles Carroll of Carrollton." It was his way of distinguishing himself from all the other Charleses in his family.

The remarkable thing about Daniel of St. Thomas Jenifer is that no one really knows why his parents, Daniel and Elizabeth Jenifer, decided to use the name St. Thomas. The family was living near Port Tobacco, Maryland, when their son was born, and they seemed intent on distinguishing him from current and future Daniels in the family (though they named a later son plain-old Daniel, causing untold grief and frustration for scores of genealogists and historians). Back then, people couldn't be certain that an infant would survive to adulthood, so they sometimes hedged their bets by giving babies in the same family the same name. This was especially important if a wealthy male child needed to have a specific name in order to come into his inheritance.

But why St. Thomas? Some historians believe this founding father was named after a local church. That's a nice thought, but the church in question was run by Catholic Jesuits, and the Jenifers raised their son in the Episcopalian faith. Others claim a Jenifer ancestor traveled through St. Thomas, in the West Indies, on his way to Maryland. Another theory holds that the Jenifer family originated on St. Thomas Island, off the coast of Cornwall, England. Nobody knows for sure.

Moreover, details of Jenifer's early years and training are sparse. As a young man, he spent his time managing his father's plantations in Charles County, Maryland. An able administrator, he branched out to work as a top "receiver general," or tax and bill collector, for the last two proprietors in Maryland. The colony had been settled by wealthy landowners who ran it like a commercial enterprise; there were no towns, cities, or local government. Basically, the proprietors (who often never set foot in America) ran their own private kingdoms and promised a cut to the English king. For these last few holdouts, Jenifer settled boundary disputes, collected rents, and paid taxes on their behalf. He did a good job, and the colonists liked him enough to give him a number of important posts. He was a justice of the peace, worked on the committee that established the Mason-Dixon Line, and became a top advisor to the last royal governor of Maryland, Sir Robert Eden.

But by 1775, when Sir Eden was ousted by patriots, Jenifer had joined the revolutionary cause and began working in Maryland's new state senate. He was assigned to Congress as well, but most of his work during the Revolutionary War exploited his talents in land management. If Maryland patriots seized a loyalist property, Jenifer managed the fallout, selling off the confiscated land and possessions, issuing the paperwork spelling out the new chain of ownership, and thus building revenue for the struggling new state. From 1782 onward, as de facto treasurer, he was one of the most powerful and best-paid office holders in the state. He wasn't among the first picks to attend the Constitutional Convention in 1787, but, after one of the four candidates backed out, Jenifer was packing his bags and heading to Philadelphia.

By now he was an affable, aristocratic sixty-four-year-old bachelor. The third oldest signer, after Ben Franklin and Roger Sherman, Jenifer attended nearly all the sessions but kept his comments to a minimum. Even though Maryland was a small state in size and population, Jenifer preferred the Virginia Plan, whereas his most prominent fellow delegate, a hard-drinking Baltimore attorney named Luther Martin, championed the New Jersey Plan. (During the most significant votes on representation, Jenifer and Martin were the only Maryland delegates in attendance; the others were likely called away to attend to other business.)

With Jenifer's and Martin's votes canceling each other out, Maryland's vote was often tied and, therefore, useless in advancing the dialogue on larger issues. Jenifer thought that the nation must have a durable, strong union and that that the federal government should have the power to tax. As an expert in governmental finance, he knew how vital sources of funding were to carrying out state business. But he was wise enough to know that the small states needed to get their way on the issue of representation or they would abandon the convention altogether.

The delegates spent most of July 2 trying to decide the make-up of the future Senate. They had already agreed that representatives in the House would be chosen according to each state's population, but then the small states began demanding equal votes in the Senate. Jenifer disagreed, but one can only assume he didn't feel too strongly about the issue because, when the time came to take a vote, he disappeared. He lingered outside the state house, certainly knowing that, without his nay vote, Martin would throw the entire state of

Signing Their Rights Away

Maryland behind equal suffrage. Minutes after the vote was taken, Jenifer ambled back into the room.

And that wasn't the only time Jenifer wouldn't get his way. On another occasion, he insisted that U.S. representatives be elected to three-year, not two-year, terms. He thought seeking election every two years would be exhausting and drive away the best office seekers. (The convention ignored his advice, and U.S. representatives still serve two-year terms.)

Jenifer would later marvel at how beautifully the delegates came together to create the Constitution. "The first month we only came to grips," he said. "And the second it seemed as though we would fly apart forever, but we didn't—we jelled."

Jenifer signed the Constitution, but his opponent Martin refused, reportedly saying, "I'll be hanged if the people support the Constitution!" Jenifer needled his convention buddy: "You should stay in Philadelphia so they don't get you with their rope!" In the end, Maryland became the seventh state to ratify the new Constitution.

The wise-cracking old land man retired to his sizable plantation estate, Stepney, where he died at the age of sixty-seven, only three years after his time in Philadelphia. Since he never did marry, Jenifer left his estate to his nephew, the plainly named Daniel, with instructions to free his slaves about six years after their master's death. Today, no one knows where the signer with the interesting middle name is buried. It's possible he was laid to rest on family property or perhaps was entombed in a famous churchyard in the Port Tobacco area that lost its headstones in a massive flood. His whereabouts, like his own odd name, are mysteries for the ages.

* * * * * * * * * * * *

Dan. Carroll

* * * * * * * * * * * *

The Signer Who Helped Create Washington, D.C.

BORN: July 22, 1730
DIED: May 7, 1796
AGE AT SIGNING: 57
PROFESSION: Merchant
BURIED: Location unknown;
   believed to be in St. John's
   Catholic Cemetery, Forest
   Glen, Maryland

* * * * * * * * * * * *

At the time of the Constitutional Convention, the nation's government was headquartered in New York City. Daniel Carroll gets a lot of the credit for moving it to the area now known as Washington, D.C. The decision was quite a controversial one back in the day, largely because Carroll's family owned much of the land that would later become the District of Columbia.

Carroll was born in Upper Marlboro, Maryland. His father—like many of the Carroll clan—was a rich planter with lots of land. He was one of seven children; his younger brother John became the first Catholic bishop and archbishop in the United States.

Hailing from one of the wealthiest families in all of the thirteen colonies did not insulate Carroll from the prejudices suffered by members of the Catholic faith, rich and poor alike. At this time in America's history, Catholics were often forbidden to practice law, build churches, or hold public office. In some colonies, Catholics who intended to assume public office were forced to take a Test Oath, renouncing their faith. Because teaching children in Catholic schools was also discouraged, Carroll was educated privately before being shipped off to France to complete his studies, an option his family could easily afford. He enrolled in a Jesuit school for six years before returning to the colonies at the age of eighteen.

Several years later Carroll's father died, leaving behind a great inheritance. Carroll then married his cousin Eleanor, thus keeping the fortune in the family while increasing his own holdings substantially, for Eleanor came with a not-too-shabby dowry of £3,000. A successful tobacco exporter, Carroll boosted his portfolio by purchasing and selling land and slaves. He also dabbled in land speculation, as did many of his fellow signers. But, luckily for him, his interest in lands west of the Appalachians did not result in complete financial ruin.

The year 1776 brought not only the start of the Revolutionary War but also the institution of the Maryland Constitution, which allowed Catholics to vote and hold office. Carroll entered the state legislature in 1777. He was not a particularly vocal or outspoken supporter of the war; some say he may even have been reluctant. Maryland hosted few battles, so residents were less likely to identify themselves as fierce loyalists or die-hard patriots. We do know, however, that Carroll purchased supplies for the army and continued to work in public office. In 1781, toward the end of the war, he was elected to Congress and ratified the Articles of Confederation on behalf of Maryland, the last of the thirteen new states to accept the governing document. In a sense, Carroll's signature put the articles into effect. That same year he entered the first Maryland state senate, where he served for many years.

He remained in Congress until 1784, when he joined with an old friend by the name of George Washington to work on the Potomac

Company. The firm sought to enhance navigation of the Potomac River by means of a canal that would help link the Mid-Atlantic states to land in the west. Since Carroll had plenty of land holdings around the river, he was eager to see the project through.

In 1787, Carroll's famous—and famously loaded—cousin Charles of Carrollton, signer of the Declaration of Independence, was asked to be a delegate to the Constitutional Convention in Philadelphia. When he declined the invitation, the opportunity fell to Daniel. He wasn't thrilled with the idea and complained of health problems. He wrote, "I dare not think of residing in Phila. in the summer months. . . . Moderate (but constant dayly) exercise, temperance and attention, have in a great measure conquer'd my nervous complaints, without the aid of Medicine."

Nevertheless, Carroll made the trip, although he arrived two months after the opening session. Though he was dreading summer in Philadelphia, he didn't let the heat and humidity stifle his performance. He apparently spoke about twenty times.

Carroll was a classic small-state nationalist. He also approved of Alexander Hamilton's idea of a strong central financial system and felt that the federal government should assume various state debts that had lingered since the war.

And, unlike many a signer with a fat wallet, Carroll was a big believer in democracy and had plenty of faith in the Everyman. Case in point: he didn't want Congress to choose the president but favored citizens electing the nation's highest office directly. He couldn't rally enough delegates to back this idea, but he eventually supported a system of presidential electors who would be chosen by the people, which would be a key component of the Electoral College system.

Carroll was one of only two Catholic signers (the other was Thomas FitzSimons of Pennsylvania). After the signing, Carroll did not take part as a delegate to his state's ratification convention, but he did help convince Maryland to ratify. He wrote articles in newspapers extolling the virtues of the new framework, calling it "the

Signing Their Rights Away

best form of government which has ever been offered to the world." He also felt that all thirteen states should be required to ratify the Constitution, but his fellow delegates overruled him. Nine were required to put the Constitution into effect, which occurred once New Hampshire ratified in 1789.

Carroll ran as a Federalist and won an appointment to the House of Representatives in the new government. Talk of amending the Constitution had already begun. He, along with Connecticut's Oliver Ellsworth and signers James Madison and William Paterson, began drafting amendments, the first ten of which became the Bill of Rights. Carroll, the Catholic signer, played a major role in drafting the first, and perhaps best-known, amendment, which guarantees, among other things, religious freedom. "Many sects have concurred in opinion that they are not well secured under the present Constitution," he said. He also contributed to the Tenth Amendment, the one that says all rights not granted to the feds are reserved for the states and the people. The Bill of Rights was added to the Constitution in 1791.

Carroll remained in the new government until 1791. He then accepted an appointment from his pal, President George Washington, to work with two other men to oversee the surveying, designing, and construction of a new federal district, which would become home to the nation's new capital. Its location, along the Potomac, was certainly fortuitous for Carroll: he owned most of the land that was designated to become Washington, D.C. This fact is largely forgotten today, but it wasn't at the time—indeed, many people questioned his impartiality.

Carroll resigned in 1795 because of poor health and died at the age of sixty-five at his home near Rock Creek. There were so many Carrolls—and a fair number of Daniels among them—that the precise location of his grave is unknown; it is believed to be in St. John's Catholic Cemetery in Forest Glen, Maryland.

IX. Virginia

★ ★ ★ ★ ★ ★ ★ ★ ★ ★ ★ ★ ★

The President of the Constitutional Convention

BORN: February 22, 1732
DIED: December 14, 1799
AGE AT SIGNING: 55
PROFESSION: Planter
BURIED: Mount Vernon Estate,
    Mount Vernon, Virginia

★ ★ ★ ★ ★ ★ ★ ★ ★ ★ ★ ★ ★

No, he never chopped down that cherry tree. That pleasant fiction was concocted by a preacher seeking to instill good moral values in America's youth. But the false teeth? George Washington definitely had those. By the time he was president he'd lost all but one of his original teeth, and so he made do with ill-fitting dentures fashioned of all kinds of crazy stuff: hippo, walrus, or elephant ivory studded with pig teeth, cow teeth, elk teeth, and even human teeth from the mouths of slaves. The falsies worked passably well, but he became self-conscious about speaking or smiling in public. That deadpan look he wears on the dollar bill was the uncomfortable result.

But don't let the dour image fool you: the father of his country was a gregarious, athletic man who loved good times, drinking, gambling, cockfights, horse races, dancing, and salty jokes. He also knew how to present a dignified self-image to the world, especially when his troops, foreign dignitaries, and the American people were watching.

Washington, the first man to sign the U.S. Constitution, was the eldest of six children of a Virginia plantation owner named Augustine and his second wife, Mary Ball Washington. Dad died when the children were young, and eleven-year-old George helped his domineering, nagging mother raise his siblings. A relatively poor child who lacked the resources to attend college, young George was mentored by his older stepbrothers. As a teen, he longed to go to sea, but his mother forbade it. He ended up becoming a surveyor and mapmaker who used his earnings and connections to acquire land. He became fascinated with the promise of frontier territories in the west and began dreaming of their possibilities. In his spare time, he rode horses, hunted, and wandered the woods in search of adventure. Despite a desire to see the world, he grew up to become a man somewhat kept, bound, hemmed in, or trapped by a life of duty and service.

Washington joined the Virginia militia when he was only about seventeen years old and served bravely during the French and Indian War in the 1750s, when Britain was battling France for control of North America. As a young lieutenant colonel, he won his first skirmish against the French in a Pennsylvania town in 1754, but later had to surrender his entire force when the French tracked them down. Released and allowed to return home, he resigned his post rather than accept a demotion. He enlisted again as an aide to British general Edward Braddock, and, though sick, he led the troops in retreat after Braddock was mortally wounded. In battle, he miraculously escaped injury countless times. Two horses were shot out from under him and bullets tore his jacket and hat to shreds, but he was unharmed. Yet, when Washington twice tried to attain an officer's post in the British army, he was rebuffed. He angrily returned home to serve in his colony's militia. A practical, tidy, and moody man with a mathematical mind and surveyor's appreciation for precision, he soon grew impatient with the disorganized way he felt the government was running the militia.

Washington quit and married a young widow, Martha Dandridge Custis, and adopted her two children. Enriched by Martha's own wealth and plantation, the young family settled at Mount Vernon, a family home Washington had inherited upon the death of his older stepbrother Lawrence. Throughout the rest of his life, even when he was at war, Washington would work at remaking the estate in his own image, establishing fields of crops, gardens, and distillery and pushing the plantation's boundaries from two thousand to eight thousand acres. (Today the famous home hosts a million tourists each year.) For a while, he embarked on the life of a fashionable Virginia planter. He dabbled in politics at the House of Burgesses, which met in Williamsburg. Though not as radical as other patriots, Washington felt that all English gentlemen were entitled to the rights abrogated by the king and Parliament and, if necessary, should be prepared to defend those rights by force. In 1775, after the shots had rung out in Lexington and Concord, he was sent to the first Continental Congress, which chose him to lead the Continental Army. And it was just as well, too. The thought of restless Washington languishing in Congress while John Adams and the others squabbled is enough to make one want to take a hatchet to a hundred fruit trees.

Washington didn't have much to work with when he took over the fledgling nation's military, but he did the best he could. Although unimpressed with the recruits, he decided they were at least worthy of training. He was a man who had once swum across a freezing river and who had crawled on his belly to scout retreat lines; he was willing to endure miserable conditions and expected the same of his men. Knowing that he was being watched, he gave them the role model that he himself would have wanted. He arrived for work in a gorgeous custom-made uniform and kept it looking spiffy throughout the battles. When times called for it, he could be tough, ordering habitual deserters hanged and others whipped.

You could say he was a good model to the congressmen back home in Philadelphia, though some schemed to oust him. Washington was nothing if not loyal to the rebel cause. When offered military wages, he declined them. He did accept roughly $65,000 in Continental currency to cover his wartime expenses, but even that money—printed on paper—lost value the longer he held it.

Only forty-three years old when he took over as commander in chief, Washington had much to learn and made a few early blunders in his defense of Brooklyn and Manhattan. By the numbers, he lost more battles than he won, but that didn't really matter, did it? He was a quick study who learned how to opportunistically pounce when he could seize the advantage. Though his troops were frequently outsupplied and outnumbered (20,000 U.S. troops to 50,000 British troops and mercenaries), Washington managed to train them into an efficient and nimble fighting force. If you had to pinpoint his military style, you could say that he worried his opponents incessantly with small battles, striking and retreating, until he found the right moment to launch a decisive attack. After he mopped Yorktown with Cornwallis's troops in 1781, the battle that won the war, Washington could have used his power to seize control of the weak U.S. government, as many of his angry unpaid soldiers wanted to do. He could have crowned himself king. But no. He addressed his troops with a few sentimental words and left them all weeping like babies. Any chance of rebellion was quashed on the spot.

When the war was over, Washington happily returned to his beloved home to rebuild his neglected finances. He managed to have a little fun, too, obsessively canoeing waterways in search of a passage to his property out west. When among friends, he let down his hair and attended parties and dinners; some historians, studying his papers, conclude that he almost never ate a meal alone. Clearly the six-foot-two general with the size thirteen shoes loved people.

Though his finances took a hit during the war, he was regarded as one of the richest men in America. But his wealth was mostly tied up in land and slaves. After the war, grateful states showed their thanks by awarding him massive tracts of land, and he added to these holdings with expensive impulse transactions. Once, on a trip to upstate New York with then governor George Clinton, he saw a huge parcel that he simply had to have. Though still owing money on other land he'd purchased, Washington proceeded to borrow $6,000 from Clinton and bought the property. Though it took him four years to repay the loan, he managed to turn a profit by selling the land in small pieces.

Washington's time off from service was exceedingly brief. In 1785, he hosted statesmen who were becoming irritated by the apparent deficiencies of the Articles of Confederation. In 1787, he went uneasily to the Constitutional Convention. He was no lawyer; what he knew was math, crops, horseflesh, and war. But his appearance in Philadelphia was necessary strategically, and he knew it. Just as he'd sported that perfect uniform, he now garbed himself as a statesman and let himself become the dignified face of the proceedings. Madison, Hamilton, James Wilson, and the others all knew that it would be impossible to dismiss the work of the delegates if the world's two most famous Americans—the libertine Dr. Franklin and the upright Gen. Washington—were in the room.

On the very first day, Washington was elected the convention's president. He took a seat at the head of the hall and apologized to those assembled. *I am not a politician,* he basically said, keeping a tight grip on his false teeth. *I lack experience, but I'll do what is asked of me.*

The men were in awe. Some had never seen him up close and were tickled to be in his presence. He need not have worried. He had them at "huzzah."

Washington didn't say much during the debates and steered clear of the legal arguments. But he was there every day, sitting in his regal chair at the head of the room. A nationalist who favored a strong government, he could have thrown himself into the arguments, and he knew the men would have forgiven his lack of legalese. But he refrained. He feared that doing so would have degraded his stature. Still, he no doubt worked miracles on reluctant members after hours, when he socialized his way through the ballrooms and taverns of Philadelphia. He also tried to convince delegates not to leave, or to return if they had. In a note to his former soldier and protégé Alexander Hamilton, he affectionately wrote, "I am sorry you went away—I wish you were back."

Not all of his communications were as sweet. In one instance, Washington discovered that one of the delegates had dropped a critical document—a copy of the Virginia Plan, which was supposed to be top secret—on his way out of the state house. The next day, Washington stood and sternly lectured the delegates about their pledge to respect the confidentiality of the proceedings, lest rumors doom the convention. He flung the papers on the desk dramatically. "I don't know whose paper it is, but here it is. Let him who owns it take it." The delegates sucked air and stared, riveted to their places. In a huff, the former general grabbed his hat and stormed out of the chambers. The papers lay unclaimed.

It never happened again.

In September, after the delegates had signed the Constitution, Washington's signature at the top of the document went a long way toward convincing Americans that they should ratify it. And no one was surprised when he was chosen to be the first president under the nation's new government. Once again his desire to be left in peace at his home in Mount Vernon was not to be. Elected in 1788, he was forced to borrow £10,000 in spending money or he never would have been able to travel to his inauguration and properly set up a second household as the nation's first chief executive.

Washington took his oath of office in 1789 and served two terms. He backed Alexander Hamilton in the establishment of a banking system, the assumption of state debts, and new tariffs to boost federal revenue; disagreements over these policies triggered the birth of political parties. Washington often had to play the peacemaker between his secretary of state Thomas Jefferson and Treasury czar Alexander Hamilton. When the Whiskey Rebellion broke out, Washington took command of troops sent to quell the uprising against an unpopular tax on hooch. This is the only time in history that a U.S. president led an army while in office.

Throughout the world and the nation, Washington was still perceived as the great liberator. He traveled around the country so that people could get a look at him. When the French stormed the Bastille on the eve of their revolution, they presented Washington the key to that notorious jail, a symbol of liberation of the political prisoners long held inside. But the irony is that, throughout his life, Washington owned slaves and made efforts to keep them as long as possible. During the early years of the presidency, when the federal government was located in Philadelphia, nine slaves worked for the president and first lady in their home in that city. At the time, any enslaved person who had lived in Philadelphia for six months was granted freedom. The Washingtons purposely rotated their staff so that no one slave would reach that critical half-year mark. Today, the site of the Washingtons' Philadelphia home, near the Liberty Bell, has been preserved as an African American heritage site.

In 1796, Washington finally got what he longed for: the chance to be an ordinary citizen once again and to return home for good. But his time at ease was brief. About three years after he left office, he fell ill with a bad cold and sore throat after working outside in snowy weather. The illness blossomed into a massive, suffocating infection that refused to abate. During his life, the grand general had beaten tuberculosis, smallpox, malaria, diphtheria, pneumonia, tonsil infections, dysentery, and bouts of dark depression. But this time he couldn't seem to shake what ailed him. Using leeches, doctors bled him of eighty ounces of blood, or 35 percent of all the blood in the human body. What a shock: he got worse, not better. Sensing the end, Washington summoned his lawyers, tended to his affairs, and made his secretary promise that he would not be buried until he lay dead three whole days. (George had once "miraculously" revived a slave who was presumed dead; he knew that people could sometimes look dead but, in fact, had not shuffled off this mortal coil.) On December 14, 1799, he died. The father of his country was sixty-six years old. He left behind a grief-stricken wife and nation as well as an estate worth more than a half million dollars. By the terms of his will, his slaves were to be freed when Martha died, which she did in 1806. Both tombs rest on the grounds of Mount Vernon.

* * * * * * * * * * * *

John Blair

* * * * * * * * * * *

The Underachieving Signer

BORN: 1732

DIED: August 31, 1800

AGE AT SIGNING: About 55

PROFESSION: Judge

BURIED: Bruton Parish Churchyard, Williamsburg, Virginia

* * * * * * * * * * *

This book features plenty of stories about the men who shaped the Constitution—men who argued passionately, men with great ideas, men who worked tirelessly for the good of the nation, staying up until all hours to improve the future of the fledgling United States.

Sadly, John Blair was not one of those men. In fact, he may have been the only signer to (1) remain absolutely silent throughout the convention and (2) abstain from serving on a single committee. About the only thing he did do was to sign his name to the final document.

Blair was born in Williamsburg, Virginia, to a wealthy and connected family. His father, John Sr., was a successful merchant and a major political player in Williamsburg, then the state capital. John

Sr. also served as president of the governor's council, or panel of advisors, and as acting governor as well. For a time, Blair's father owned Raleigh Tavern, a legendary meeting place for Virginia patriots. Washington was a regular patron of the watering hole, and the nonimportation agreement against Britain was drafted on its tables. As nineteenth-century journalist Benjamin Lossing described it, "The Raleigh Tavern and the Apollo Room are to Virginia, relatively, what Faneuil Hall is to Massachusetts."

The red-headed Blair's political pedigree and advantages led him to study law at prestigious Middle Temple in London, then a popular choice for well-to-do colonists. While there, he met and married Jean Balfour, and the couple went on to have two daughters. When he returned home to Williamsburg, he joined the bar and started his own practice.

Blair's introduction into politics came in 1766, via the House of Burgesses, where he held the seat designated for the College of William and Mary. He didn't support every item on the revolutionary agenda and probably seemed mild compared to stauncher Virginia patriots, like Patrick Henry. In fact, Blair opposed Henry's resolutions to denounce the notorious Stamp Act.

But it wasn't long before Blair had changed his mind. When the royal governor, Lord Botetourt, dissolved the House of Burgesses in 1769 as punishment for their protest against acts of the British government, Blair's opinions became more firmly aligned with those of his Virginia compatriots, Henry and Washington. However, the exiled burgesses would not be dissuaded. Despite their disbandment, they held their own meetings at Raleigh Tavern; it was during this time that they signed the agreement boycotting the importation of British goods until the taxes were repealed. Later in the year, they were called back into session by Botetourt. That same year the British repealed the Townshend Acts, which levied taxes on glass, lead, paints, and paper, but did not lift the most lucrative tax, on tea.

Though he never participated in the Continental Congress or fight during the Revolutionary War, Blair served on the Privy

Council, an advisory group, for his state's first governor, Patrick Henry. In 1778, Blair advanced from lawyer to judge, serving first on the general court of Virginia and eventually rising to the post of chief justice. He then moved on to the Virginia High Court of Chancery, where he served alongside famed legal scholar (and Declaration of Independence signer) George Wythe. Blair was also a member of Virginia's first court of appeals.

Despite a couple notable absences from Virginia's delegation to the Constitutional Convention in 1787—Jefferson was busy in Paris; Patrick Henry declined to attend because he "smelt a rat"—the group was an impressive one. George Mason, George Wythe, then-governor Edmund Randolph, James Madison, George Washington—all were big names with equally large revolutionary reps. Yet, despite the enormity of the state, both in population and in revolutionary clout, only three men ultimately signed the Constitution for Virginia: Madison, Washington, and little-known Blair; the other four did not sign.

Despite his attendance at the convention, Blair was all but invisible. He made no speeches and served on no committees. About his only memorable moment came at the end, when he was traveling home with George Washington and one of the horses pulling their carriage fell through the bottom of an old bridge. Had the other horse gone through as well, Washington wrote, he "would have taken the carriage along with him." Fortunately, the men escaped unharmed and headed back home, where the battle for ratification awaited.

As a member of the York County delegation, Blair attended Virginia's ratifying convention in support of the Constitution. The state barely passed, thanks to strong anti-Federalist feelings, many embodied by the fiery Patrick Henry, who declared:

> That this is a consolidated Government is demonstrably clear, and the danger of such a Government, is, to my mind, very striking. I have the highest veneration of those Gentlemen, —but, Sir, give me

leave to demand, what right had they to say, 'We the People'? My political curiosity, exclusive of my anxious solicitude for the public welfare, leads me to ask who authorised them to speak the language of, 'We the People,' instead of 'We the States'? States are the characteristics, and the soul of a confederation. If the States be not the agents of this compact, it must be one great consolidated National Government of the people of all the States.

But by this time, the Constitution was already in effect, thanks to New Hampshire's ratification, and none of Henry's bluster could halt the momentum. Virginia became the tenth state to ratify, with a vote of 89 to 79.

Soon afterward, Washington appointed Blair an associate justice of the Supreme Court, but his role in the high court was short-lived. He resigned in 1796 because of illness. In his final years, he suffered a great pain, describing what sounds much like a stroke: "All at once a torpid numbness seized my whole face and I found my intellectual powers much weakened and all was confusion."

Blair died in 1800. His hometown of Williamsburg is a must-see for historians of all backgrounds. To commune with his spirit, you can visit the John Blair House and Kitchen within Historic Williamsburg, stop by Raleigh Tavern (rebuilt in 1932 after an 1859 fire), or visit Blair's grave, located in Bruton Parish Churchyard.

★ ★ ★ ★ ★ ★ ★ ★ ★ ★ ★ ★

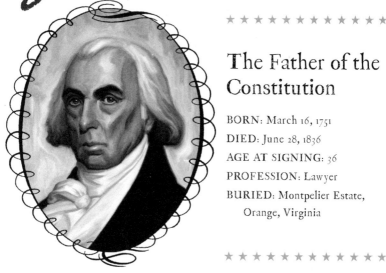

James Madison Jr

* * * * * * * * * * * *

The Father of the Constitution

BORN: March 16, 1751
DIED: June 28, 1836
AGE AT SIGNING: 36
PROFESSION: Lawyer
BURIED: Montpelier Estate,
   Orange, Virginia

* * * * * * * * * * * *

little man with big ideas—standing between five-foot-two and five-foot-six and weighing maybe a hundred pounds soaking wet—James Madison has the distinction of being the shortest president in U.S. history. But what he lacked in stature and even in personality (the guy was dry as toast), he made up for in ideas and conviction.

Madison grew up on his father's plantation, Montpelier, in Orange County, Virginia, and enjoyed every advantage offered to children of the planter aristocracy. Boarding school and tutors led to study at the College of New Jersey (now Princeton University), where, after completing his degree, he stayed on a year to study theology. He had the added benefit of studying under John Witherspoon, then president of the college, who went on to be the only practicing clergyman to sign the Declaration of Independence. Madison didn't have the lungs for preaching, and though he had studied law—the profession of choice for well-bred sons of planters—that avenue didn't appeal to him, either. He never needed to work or hold down a job and was not interested in following in his father's footsteps in the planter world. What did appeal to him were books and government. Throughout his education and his life, he learned everything there was to know about political theory, governments past and present, plus some ancient philosophy, for good measure.

Madison is often described by historians as "frail" and "sickly," but modern assessments of his health suggest the illnesses from which he suffered were both real and imagined. He was a prematurely bald young man who utilized a comb-over to conceal a shiny pate. Shy and soft-spoken, he was incessantly referred to as "modest" by anyone who knew him (these are not the usual traits that spring to mind when one thinks of a career politician). He joined the revolutionary cause early on but did not serve actively in the militia. Instead, he joined Orange County's Committee of Safety in 1775 and, the next year, attended the Virginia Convention, where he helped write that state's first constitution. He later entered the legislature and served on the Council of State.

Madison also served on the advisory committees to two famed Virginia governors, Patrick Henry and Thomas Jefferson; the latter would become a lifelong friend. When Madison finally went to Congress the year was 1780, and he was the youngest man there. This was the era of the Articles of Confederation—the precursor to the Constitution—and during this period Madison played a role in structuring the government. He soon cultivated a friendship with fellow nationalist Alexander Hamilton.

Upon returning to the Virginia legislature in 1784, Madison began writing in various capacities about the limits of the Articles of Confederation; one of his most famous works is a document titled "Vices of the Political System of the United States" (otherwise known as "Madison's Vices"). When he attended the Mount Vernon Conference (which was convened to help settle disputes between Virginia and Maryland over the navigation of the Potomac River),

Madison became even more convinced that the articles were not cutting the colonial mustard. He knew that more disagreements between states would be inevitable—and that a strong national legislature was needed to keep things in check. The conference, held at George Washington's plantation, was a precursor to the Annapolis Convention, where Madison connected once more with Hamilton; the pair helped convince everyone that Congress should put out a call to the states to send delegates to Philadelphia and iron out a new system of government.

Madison arrived in Philadelphia with a vast knowledge of governments and their shortcomings. Indeed, he had spent most of his thirty-six years preparing for this moment. He arrived early, checked into a boarding house, and began taking notes, many of which would form the basis for the Virginia Plan, which, in turn, would help shape the Constitution.

Madison had some very real concerns about power and human frailty. He believed that "human beings are generally governed by rather base and selfish motives, by suspicion, jealousy, desire for self-aggrandizement, and disinclination to do more than is required by convenience or self-interest, or exacted of them by force." This was a not-too-subtle jab at human nature by a guy who rarely raised his voice. He was also wary of interest groups and, like many of the framers, feared mob mentality. He felt the need to keep power in check and once observed, "You must first enable the government to control the governed; and in the next place, oblige it to control itself."

Madison had a number of other concrete ideas: The national government should tax citizens directly. Representation should be proportional to population. The national government should be able to veto state legislation. The chief executive of this national government should not have as much power as the legislative body. Yet, for all his fears, he took comfort in the fact that the aforementioned interest groups would have a tough time gaining momentum strong enough to disrupt government, because the country was so large and everyone was so spread out and—don't forget—it took weeks for a letter to get from one place to another. (His frail little body would have collapsed into a quivering heap at the thought of what today's special-interest groups can accomplish on the Internet.)

On the very first day of the convention, Madison requested permission from Washington to sit at the front of the room, with his back to the general, so he could take notes. Washington obliged. Despite his low, virtually-impossible-to-hear voice, Madison spoke at least 150 times at the convention, bested in speech count only by James Wilson and Gouverneur Morris. He also served on the important Committee of Style and that of Postponed Matters.

In the end, the Virginia Plan was modified by the Great Compromise, which pleased Madison not at all. He signed the document with his tiny signature, adding a "Jr" after his name. All in all, the convention did not go the way he had hoped. But the copious, detailed notes that he took, along with the outline for government that he helped shape into the Virginia Plan and his tireless urging to hold the Constitutional Convention in the first place, helped establish him as a primary—if not *the* primary—force behind the modern U.S. government.

But the convention was only half the battle.

Back home in Virginia, Madison had to confront antinationalists and political power players, such as George Mason, Patrick "I smelt a rat" Henry, and Richard Henry Lee, all of whom were against ratifying the Constitution. Madison fought hard at home and, with Alexander Hamilton and John Jay, helped author the "Federalist Papers," a series of essays published in New York newspapers and beyond that explained and defended the concepts inherent in the Constitution. Virginia became the tenth state to ratify, squeaking by with a vote of 89 to 79.

Madison was eager to serve as a senator in the new government, but Patrick Henry would have none of it. After Henry publicly criticized him as "unworthy of the confidence of the people," Madison fell short in votes.

Madison then turned his attention to the House of

Representatives, where once again Henry tried to thwart him, but this time Madison prevailed; he beat James Monroe and served in the new government from 1789 to 1797. While there, he worked to fulfill the promise he had made during Virginia's ratification battle: to get cracking on a Bill of Rights. He served as chair of the committee that drafted that document. He helped organize the executive branch of government and the federal taxation system. He began to sour on Alexander Hamilton's policies and found himself increasingly sympathetic to those of his friend and Virginia neighbor, Thomas Jefferson. (Monticello and Montpelier are less than thirty miles apart.) The pair united, and together they created the Democratic-Republican Party.

All of this studying, writing, and politicking hadn't left Madison with much time for socializing, and it's doubtful that many women found his quiet, almost skittish behavior very appealing. Nevertheless, he had the spectacular good sense to marry Dolley Payne, a woman who had lost her first husband to yellow fever. The two were the ultimate odd couple—she was vivacious and outgoing; he was, well, not. But theirs appears to have been a true love.

When Jefferson took office as president in 1801, he appointed Madison his secretary of state. It was a tricky time for diplomacy. There were still troubles with theft and piracy on the high seas, diplomacy and sanctions seemed to be doing little good, and folks feared another war was brewing—this time involving the North African Barbary States. During this time, Dolley often played hostess at the White House, since Jefferson had lost his wife, Martha. It turned out to be good practice for Dolley; when Madison became the country's fourth president, serving from 1809 to 1817, she took on the role as one of the most celebrated first ladies (and, as every schoolkid knows, the first to serve ice cream in the White House).

But times were tough. The Napoleonic Wars were raging in Europe, and tensions with Britain erupted into the War of 1812. The First Lady demonstrated her heroism when the British army invaded Washington D.C.; she wrote her sister several letters describing what would turn out

Signing Their Rights Away

to be an invaluable act of bravery and level-headedness: "I have pressed as many cabinet papers into trunks as to fill one carriage; our private property must be sacrificed, as it is impossible to procure wagons for its transportation. . . . Our kind friend, Mr. Carroll, has come to hasten my departure, and is in a very bad humor with me, because I insist on waiting until the large picture of General Washington is secured, and it requires to be unscrewed from the wall. . . . I have ordered the frame to be broken and the canvass taken out." And so it is thanks to Dolley Madison that some of the White House's most precious papers, as well as Gilbert Stuart's famed portrait of George Washington, have survived.

The Treaty of Ghent brought a wimpy end to the stalemate of a war, though Andrew Jackson's triumph in the battle of New Orleans—which technically occurred after the conflict's end—perhaps gave the United States a false feeling of victory.

Madison retired to Montpelier but remained politically active. He was cochair of the Virginia Constitutional Convention, took on the post of foreign-policy advisor to President James Monroe, and served as rector (or president) of the University of Virginia. He dedicated time to editing his journals, including his notes from the Constitutional Convention, leaving instructions that they not be published until after his death. They were published in 1836 and remain the best guide to the extraordinary events of that remarkable summer in 1787.

The house and grounds of Madison's Montpelier, in Virginia, are open to the public and currently undergoing renovations. The Octagon House in Washington, D.C., where the Madisons lived after the burning of the White House and where the Treaty of Ghent was signed, is also open to visitors.

* * * * * * * * * * * * *

Virginia

X. North Carolina

The Signer Who ... Oh, There's No Way to Dance Around the Issue, This Guy Was a Crook

BORN: March 26, 1749
DIED: March 21, 1800
AGE AT SIGNING: 38
PROFESSION: Planter, politician
BURIED: First Presbyterian
       Church, Knoxville, Tennessee

★ ★ ★ ★ ★ ★ ★ ★ ★ ★ ★

Scoundrel. Rogue. Rascal. Scalawag. Rapscallion. There are so many delicious words in the English language to describe the less-savory side of William Blount that it can be easy to forget that—regardless of his motives—this shady signer was instrumental in getting North Carolina to ratify the Constitution.

Raised at Blount Hall, a large cotton and tobacco plantation near then colonial capital of New Bern, North Carolina, Blount (pronounced *blunt*) was the eldest of a large brood. His father, Jacob, was a prosperous merchant who was active in land acquisition. The Blount children were taught primarily by tutors and their parents. Blount lost his mother, Barbara Gray, when he was fourteen years old; as the eldest in the family, he stayed close to his father and learned all there was to know about buying and selling property. These lessons would contribute equally to his successes as well as his failures.

In 1776, with the Revolutionary War raging, Blount was appointed regimental paymaster for the Third North Carolina Regiment and, later, chief paymaster of state forces and deputy paymaster general for North Carolina. Under General Horatio Gates, head of the southern armies, Blount served as a chief commissary agent, a handy post for a budding wheeler-dealer in which he handled purchasing and supplies. After the brief but brutal and bloody defeat at Camden, South Carolina, Gates hightailed it from the battlefield; he left behind not only weapons but, supposedly, £300,000 in paper currency, a sum intended for the soldier's payroll, which Blount later reported to the federal government as, *ahem*, "missing."

Blount married Mary Grainger in 1778, and in 1780 he left the military and began his political career as part of the North Carolina state legislature. He was appointed to the Continental Congress in 1782 but the next year decided to return home, serving again as part of the state legislature and working to expand his already considerable land holdings.

Blount, with his brother John Gray Blount, had his hands in literally millions of acres, and together they worked via the North Carolina legislature to open to settlement the lands west of the Appalachian Mountains. Trading posts were established, and Blount secured an appointment as an agent dealing with the Native American tribes on the frontier, in hopes of ensuring that any treaties struck would favor his extensive interests in the area. Blount wasn't always successful in convincing other members of the commission to give up more land to speculators, but that didn't stop him from getting creative with his purchases. He used aliases, took land that wasn't legally his, and deceived Native Americans along the way. These actions certainly didn't make him a leading candidate for any ethics awards, but they did keep him popular among settlers who had similar goals but lacked Blount's talent for chicanery.

In 1786, Blount was back in the Continental Congress and traveled to New York to talk up the importance of encouraging migration toward the frontier; he even put mentions in newspapers in London and New York encouraging folks to do just that—a ploy that would increase the value of his own holdings. The next year, he then served as a delegate to the Constitutional Convention in Philadelphia. He didn't speak much during the convention, nor did he hold much faith in the future of the United States. Though delegates were forbidden to do so, Blount sent home letters in which he discussed the deliberations, expressing his pessimism in this way: "We shall ultimately and not many years hence be separated and distinct governments perfectly independent of each other." Although reluctant at first to sign the Constitution, he later explained away why he did so, hedging that his signature was not technically a mark of approval but merely proof of his presence at the proceedings.

Eventually, Blount came to support the idea of a strong central government, if only because it would ease the way for westward expansion. But North Carolina would prove to be a tough anti-Federalist nut to crack—citizens of the state were demanding a Bill of Rights. Blount's lobbying in favor of ratification didn't win him many fans; he was not elected as a delegate to the state's convention in 1788, and ratification was handily rejected. But by the next year, after ratification by nine other states and with the Constitution officially in effect, Blount's arguments suddenly seemed more compelling. Another convention was held, this time with Federalists driving the conversation. On November 21, 1789, North Carolina became the twelfth state, leaving as the last holdout only Rhode Island, which hadn't even participated in the Constitutional Convention.

The next year, President Washington appointed Blount governor for the Territory of the United States South of the River Ohio, a region that included Tennessee and parts of western North

Carolina. Blount was also superintendent of Indian affairs for the southern department and, in that role, negotiated treaties with such tribes as the Creek, Cherokee, Choctaw, and Chickasaw. He organized militia and also swore in a twenty-three-year-old upstart named Andrew Jackson as attorney general for the western part of territory. His opportunities on the development front were staggering. Let the wild land-speculating rumpus begin!

In 1792 Blount began constructing Blount Mansion in Knoxville, which he decided would be the territory's new capital. In 1796, he was president of the convention that made Tennessee the sixteenth state and was elected one of its first two senators. Knoxville served as state capital until 1817.

Then things went horribly wrong.

Blount and his brother had millions of acres to their name (or any of the fictitious monikers they used at the time). With ongoing wars in Europe causing immigration to dry up, land values took a swan dive. Ever crafty, Blount became involved in a nutty plan to incite Native American wars with Spanish territories in Louisiana, Florida, and beyond. In the letter that sealed his fate, he wrote that his role would be "at the head of the business on the part of the British." Whoops. He instructed his correspondent to burn this incriminating letter after reading it; instead, the missive found its way into the hands of President John Adams, who turned it over to the Senate, which charged Blount with treason and conspiracy. The House impeached him, and the Senate promptly gave Blount the boot. He tried fleeing Philadelphia but was stopped and his possessions were seized. He posted bond and was set to stand trial before the U.S. Senate but escaped to North Carolina, where he hid from his government and his creditors.

Eventually, Blount made his way home to Tennessee, where he remained as popular as ever. So much so that, when the impeachment trial was about to begin, the Senate was forced to send a sergeant at arms down to Knoxville to arrest the wily fugitive and drag him back to Philadelphia; Blount wined him, dined him, and declined him. He hired attorneys—including his fellow Constitution signer Jared Ingersoll—to represent him at the trial, but the Senate ended up dismissing all charges.

Though Blount was the first person ever impeached in the United States, his popularity at home remained intact, and he served in the Tennessee legislature until his death, in 1800, at age fifty. Today you can visit his stately home, Blount Mansion, in Knoxville, Tennessee.

* * * * * * * * * * * *

Rich? Dobbs Spaight.

★ ★ ★ ★ ★ ★ ★ ★ ★ ★ ★ ★

The *Other* Signer Who Died in a Duel

BORN: March 25, 1758
DIED: September 6, 1802
AGE AT SIGNING: 29
PROFESSION: Planter, politician
BURIED: Clermont Estate
    Cemetery, New Bern,
    North Carolina

★ ★ ★ ★ ★ ★ ★ ★ ★ ★ ★ ★

Richard Dobbs Spaight was a true son of North Carolina. Of the five men sent to represent the Tar Heel State at the Constitutional Convention, only two had been born there. William Blount was the scoundrel. Spaight was the hero—a man the people would someday elevate to the office of governor. And, like many storied sons of the South, he died a tragic if honorable death.

Spaight was born in the coastal town of New Bern, North Carolina. His mother, Margaret Dobbs, was the sister of the royal governor, and his wealthy planter father, Richard, was the governor's secretary. One by one they all died—the governor, his sister, and her husband—and the poor little rich kid was shipped off to Great Britain by his guardians. When the Revolutionary War broke out, young

Spaight was studying at the University of Glasgow, but upon graduation he made the trek back home to serve on the patriot side as an administrative officer to the North Carolina militia. He fought in the battle of Camden, South Carolina, a major defeat for the colonies, and achieved the rank of lieutenant colonel. Blessed with youth, looks, wealth, and a fine war record, he went into local politics and was sent to Congress at the end of the war. Spaight, who owned seventy-one slaves, drew Thomas Jefferson's ire when he worked to kill a bill that would have ended slavery in the western half of the growing nation. Jefferson never forgave him and would later speak of him as the man who let slavery spread westward. Before the age of thirty, Spaight was speaker of his state legislature, a post that sent him to the Constitutional Convention.

Like many of the delegates, Spaight was an aristocrat and had little faith in the common people to elect their leaders; he also suggested that the president and senators each serve seven years, an idea that was quickly nixed. (U.S. presidents are elected for terms of four years, senators for six.) But when he suggested that senators be chosen by state legislatures, the convention seized upon the idea. And that was how senators were chosen until 1913, when the Seventeenth Amendment was adopted and provided for them to be elected directly by the American people. Spaight also wanted the president to be chosen by Congress, an idea borrowed from the Virginia Plan. The framers, generally fearful of mob rule, tended toward inserting checks into the system to correct for a bad popular decision. Hence, they created an electoral college, which would be based on a proportion of the popular vote, to select the president. Spaight never missed a session of the convention and signed the Constitution on September 17.

But for almost two years North Carolina waffled on ratifying the document. To bring about resolution, Spaight convinced his friend George Washington to visit and use his considerable influence to sway votes. Spaight himself probably would have spent more time campaigning for ratification, but he was forced to take a breather from politicking because of poor health. No one knows what ailed him. He was only twenty-nine when the convention concluded and may have suffered from a disease, congenital defect, or health condition not identifiable by medical techniques of the day. He tried traveling to the West Indies to recuperate but returned home by 1792, when he was elected to be his state's first locally born governor. An honest, conscientious leader, he moved the state capital to Raleigh and was instrumental in the founding of the university at Chapel Hill. When his term ended in 1795, the thirty-seven-year-old former governor married Mary Leach, a Yankee woman from Pennsylvania. They had three children.

For the next few years, Spaight tried his best to stay active in state and national politics, but his mysterious health issues continued to interfere. He was elected to the House of Representatives for one term, and then a second, but was forced to take leaves of absence. He finally threw in the towel in 1801, after supporting Thomas Jefferson for president. He resigned himself to staying close to home in the state senate. His Federalist opponent, John Stanly, who landed the seat Spaight vacated in Congress, proceeded to badmouth his predecessor. Spaight was not sickly, Stanly claimed, but had merely used his health as an excuse to avoid taking a stand on controversial issues. The ailing Spaight—he of the perfect convention attendance—defended himself with angry handbills distributed to voters.

The situation got ugly and ended with the two men meeting at dawn with pistols drawn. Although today duels may seem like a foolish way to settle an argument, in colonial times they were a handy means of preventing a disagreement from blossoming into an all-out feud between families. Duels also preserved men's honor. If they showed up, fired their pistols, and made it obvious they didn't want to kill anyone, they could emerge with their reputations intact.

But sometimes the duelers were out for blood—and such was the case when Spaight met Stanly in New Bern, North Carolina.

Spaight's biographers claim that he was so sickly he could barely hold his pistol. He was no match for the healthier Stanly, who fired four shots, hitting his opponent with his last round. Spaight died the next day, leaving behind his wife and children. He was only forty-four years old. Stanly faced a murder rap but was pardoned by the governor. All told, three significant founding fathers lost their lives in duels: Button Gwinnett, a Georgia signer of the Declaration of Independence; Alexander Hamilton; and the little-known Spaight.

The late governor was buried on the grounds of his mother-in-law's 2,500-acre estate, Clermont. Unfortunately, Union soldiers plundered and burned the plantation house to the ground in 1862. According to local legend, Yankee looters also desecrated Spaight's grave; they stole his casket, spilled his skeleton onto the ground, and hung his skull on the gatepost. His coffin was allegedly used to ship the body of a Union soldier back north. Today the family plot, which contains the graves of eleven Spaight family members, is located on a lonely country road—and is enclosed on all sides by a tall brick wall and a heavy iron gate.

* * * * * * * * * * * *

Hu Williamson (signature)

★ ★ ★ ★ ★ ★ ★ ★ ★ ★ ★

The Signer Who
Believed in Aliens

BORN: December 5, 1735
DIED: May 22, 1819
AGE AT SIGNING: 51
PROFESSION: Doctor,
   merchant, minister, scientist
BURIED: Trinity Churchyard,
   New York, New York

★ ★ ★ ★ ★ ★ ★ ★ ★ ★ ★

In the eighteenth century, the night skies were a constant source of wonder, and many founding fathers studied them carefully—especially Hugh Williamson, the last man to sign the Constitution for the state of North Carolina. He never claimed to have witnessed an extraterrestrial, but he was nonetheless convinced that the heavens were teeming with intelligent life.

Williamson was born in Chester County, Pennsylvania, to a pair of Scotch-Irish parents who had immigrated to America to run a clothing business. Young Hugh was studious and serious, but, judging from his zigzagging career path, he could have used a good guidance counselor. He began divinity studies in 1759 and worked for about two years as a licensed Presbyterian minister, though he was never formally ordained. Then he switched to mathematics and landed a professorship at his alma mater, the future University of Pennsylvania. Three years after that, he quit that post and dashed over to the Continent, where he studied medicine in Scotland, England, and the Netherlands. By about 1768, as the colonies were embroiled in taxation disputes with the motherland, Williamson was back in Philadelphia, working as a doctor and observing the stars in his spare time.

A frequent correspondent of fellow astronomy geek Ben Franklin, Williamson studied comets and announced to the world that their tails were not fire, but a reflection of sunlight. (Today we know that comet tails are in fact gas and dust, which, yes, reflect sunlight.) Extrapolating from his theory, Williamson wrongly concluded that all planets and comets had mild enough climates to permit life. "Having ventured the opinion that every planet and every comet in our system is inhabited," he wrote, "we have only taken a very imperfect view of the astonishing works of the divine architect."

He quickly did some math and arrived at the conclusion that there are no fewer than "five millions of worlds, all inhabited by rational beings." The hugeness of that number impressed him, and he made the same observation that generations of scientists have since also made when contemplating the vastness of the universe: "How do we seem to dwindle into littleness! How small, how few, are the ephemerons of this little globe, when compared with the countless myriads who inhabit five millions of worlds!" Because he was a devout man, Williamson drew a swift connection between science and God. "All these worlds, and every one of their inhabitants, are under the constant care of the Divine Being," he wrote. "Not one of them is neglected. 'Great and marvelous' are his works, how terrible his power!!"

Williamson had many interests beyond astronomy. In the early 1770s, he became a trustee of the Academy of Newark, Delaware, which wanted to become a full-fledged college. The school appointed Williamson as fund-raiser, and he traveled throughout the colonies and England to raise money. Over the course of his journey,

Williamson observed growing political unrest. He witnessed the Boston Tea Party, and, when later he arrived in London, he was summoned to testify before the British Privy Council, an advisory body to the Crown. He warned the council that further pressure on the colonists would result in rebellion.

Williamson then proceeded to do something extremely foolhardy and treasonous. While still in England, he posed as a British official, bluffed his way into intercepting letters from the Massachusetts royal governor, and passed them on to Ben Franklin, who published them as proof that the governor was conspiring with Parliament to curtail the rights of colonists. Franklin, who was living in England at the time, would take the blame for stealing the letters; until his death, no one ever knew that Williamson had in fact been the spy.

Williamson headed home in 1777, but by then war was raging and his ship was seized by British troops. He and another man managed to elude capture by swiping a lifeboat, lowering it to the water, and rowing themselves to shore. He abandoned his life in Philadelphia and relocated to the town of Edenton, North Carolina, where he worked as a merchant and physician. He soon entered the state militia as a military surgeon and, following a rout by British forces in South Carolina, volunteered to cross enemy lines to care for American prisoners of war. On that mission and others, Williamson distinguished himself by keeping a careful eye on food, water, and hygiene. He managed to keep those troops in his care free from contagion for the duration of his service, no mean feat in the Carolina swamps.

His new neighbors chose him to serve in North Carolina's legislature in 1782, a year before the war ended. His colleagues there sent him to Congress and the convention in May 1787. He seemed a good match for the other profound thinkers who had assembled to hammer out a new constitution; Thomas Jefferson praised Williamson's "acute mind" and "high degree of erudition." Indeed, Williamson was the most active and vocal of the three North Carolina delegates. As the group debated the composition of Congress under the new constitution, he insisted that the "aristocratic" branch—then code for the future U.S. Senate—should hold the nation's purse strings and vote on taxes; he didn't think the common people represented by the lower branch—the House—would wisely spend tax revenue. This proposal was shot down by George Mason of Virginia, who asked, in effect: *Where would the money come from? The common people, that's who! Aristocrats will soon forget where the money is coming from, spend poorly, and there will be tyranny.* Although this proposal was rejected, we know at least one of Williamson's contributions to the Constitution made it all the way to the final draft: the six-year term for U.S. senators.

By then a prickly fifty-three-year-old bachelor who did not suffer fools and flatterers gladly, Williamson found love with a wealthy twenty-one-year-old New Yorker named Maria Apthorp. They married in 1789, but Apthorp died only a few years later, after the birth of the couple's second son. The tragedy may have blunted Williamson's relentless productivity; after three years in the new Congress under President George Washington, he moved back to his late wife's beloved Manhattan to educate his sons and indulge his own love of learning.

In his retirement, Williamson dabbled in science, wrote books and research papers, volunteered at hospitals, engaged in philanthropy, and never stopped staring up at the stars. When Maria's father died in 1797, Williamson dutifully handled financial affairs on behalf of the large Apthorp family, and eventually he bought for his sons a section of the two-hundred-acre estate in Bloomingdale, a rural suburb in what is now the Upper West Side of Manhattan. The framer lived another twenty-four years, until his death in 1819, at age eighty-three. He is buried in his wife's family plot in New York City, right at the head of Wall Street. The stone covering the spot bears the Apthorp name and makes no mention of the versatile man who loved religion, stars, math, and statesmanship, all with equal passion.

XI. South Carolina

[signature: J. Rutledge]

The Signer Who Attempted Suicide

BORN: September, 1739
DIED: July 18, 1800
AGE AT SIGNING: About 48
PROFESSION: Lawyer
BURIED: St. Michael's Church
    Cemetery, Charleston, South
    Carolina

★ ★ ★ ★ ★ ★ ★ ★ ★ ★ ★ ★

*H*e defended Charleston during the Revolutionary War, chaired the committee that created the first draft of the U.S. Constitution, and even enjoyed a short stint as chief justice of the Supreme Court. But none of these achievements could shield John Rutledge from the tragic depression that would make him try to take his own life.

The Rutledge, Pinckney, and Middleton dynasties were to South Carolina what the Kennedys would later be to Massachusetts: moneyed first families of politicians and lawmakers. This trio of South Carolina families—which associated socially and intermarried—contributed five signers to the two most significant documents in American history. Of the lot, John Rutledge was perhaps the most eloquent and legally brilliant. His life, both political and personal, took its fair share of nose-dives over the years, but through it all he remained dedicated to the country whose government he played a crucial part in framing. How else can you explain the fact that he named his son States?

Rutledge was born in Charleston to an Irish immigrant and a well-established doctor. His mother, only fifteen years old when she married, was reputedly the wealthiest heiress in the colony. Rutledge's early life was spent with tutors and at the library. He lost his father when he was only eleven and began spending time at his uncle Andrew's law office, studying what would become his life's work. His uncle was also speaker of the lower house of the South Carolina legislature, which gave Rutledge the chance to observe his second calling: politics. He would watch the debates whenever he could. Later, Rutledge studied law at the prestigious Middle Temple in London. On his return to Charleston, he learned that his uncle had died and his mother needed help managing the estate. He took primary responsibility for the education of his younger brothers, Edward and Hugh, and funded the completion of their studies in England.

In 1761, at only twenty-one years old, Rutledge became a member of the South Carolina legislature. His reputation as a lawyer had already begun to take hold, with rumors of his winning streaks in court growing like the size of a wide-mouthed bass after a long, drunken fishing trip. He married Elizabeth Grimké, a planter's daughter, in 1763, and the pair ultimately had ten children (the last of whom was named after a political-geographical designation). At the tender age of twenty-five, he was appointed the state's attorney general.

On the national stage, Rutledge's first gig was the Stamp Act Congress, in 1765, in New York, where representatives gathered to decide how to respond to the paper-and-documents tax imposed on them. Rutledge made an impression as the youngest attendee. When South Carolina's royal governor dismissed the legislature in 1774, Rutledge and others formed the Committee of Public Safety, a rebel watchdog group, and met in alternate locations.

That same year, Rutledge was head of the delegation to the first Continental Congress. John Adams had already taken note of him, writing, "John Rutledge still maintains that air of reserve, design, and cunning." Adams credited Rutledge with helping to unify the otherwise disparate views of the delegates.

When Rutledge returned to the Second Continental Congress, he served on a number of committees; but as time wore on, he saw that the situation between the loyalists and the patriots in South Carolina was worsening. He returned to Charleston. Meanwhile, his younger brother Edward went on to sign the Declaration of Independence.

Back in Charleston, Rutledge chaired the committee that drafted South Carolina's constitution, which he also helped to write. The legislature also elected him as the first president of the lower house of the assembly and commander of the state's military. Though Rutledge was a moderate who believed in peacefully solving problems with those across the pond, if possible, he was always prepared to take things to the next level. That moment came in 1776, as British troops parked themselves off Sullivan's Island, just outside Charleston, and were ready to fire on a fort under the command of Colonel William Moultrie. Washington's own commander, Major General Charles Lee, thought Moultrie and the others should evacuate. Rutledge, the supposed moderate, disagreed. He reminded Moultrie that he, Rutledge, was the only one who could draft the order to evacuate, adding, "I would sooner cut off my hand than write one." As it turned out, the bombing by the British was ineffectual against the palmetto logs used to build the fort. Moreover, American sharpshooters fared well against the sitting ducks offshore, fatally wounding Lord William Campbell, whom the British intended to put back in charge as royal governor. The fleet tucked tail and left. The Sabal palmetto—a hero of the encounter—remains the state tree of South Carolina and is prominently featured on its flag.

Though he had run-ins with political opponents, Rutledge was elected the first governor of South Carolina and exercised such free reign that some referred to him as "Dictator John." Dictator or no, his primary concern was recruiting militia and otherwise prepping Charleston for the coming Redcoat onslaught. When the city finally fell to the British in 1780, his estate was seized and Rutledge escaped to North Carolina, thus avoiding capture. As a man with money, property in town, and plantations, he had much to lose. His public duties were costing him a lot, and there was little income when he had no time to practice law.

Rutledge retired as governor in 1782, and his brother-in-law John Matthews took over. In 1782 and '83, Rutledge served as a congressional delegate, this time to the Congress of the Confederation, and in 1784 he was judge of the chancery court in South Carolina, a position he held for seven years. He liked seeing cases resolved speedily, saying, "Delayed justice is injustice." Unlike his brother Edward, he was not a man about town, flitting around Charleston's buzzing social scene, but was well regarded on the national level as a man of integrity.

In 1787, Rutledge was off to Philadelphia for the Constitutional Convention. His reputation as a barrister and governor preceded him, and he arrived as a major player (he seconded the nomination of Washington as president). He spoke often and convincingly— and not infrequently in defense of the slave trade; he is at least partly responsible for keeping any prohibitive language regarding slavery out of the Constitution. He chaired the five-person Committee of Detail, responsible for drafting the Constitution, and is considered a major contributor to the document.

Rutledge was in favor of wealth-based representation, wanted the sessions to be kept secret until their conclusion, and understood the meaning of the word *compromise*, though he may not have always been happy with the outcome: "Is it not better that I should sacrifice one prized opinion than that all of us should sacrifice everything we might otherwise gain?" After signing the Constitution, he returned to South Carolina to lobby for ratification; the vote passed with a healthy margin of 149 to 73, making his state the eighth to endorse the document.

When John Jay, chief justice of the U.S. Supreme Court, retired in 1795, Rutledge was quick to let Washington know that he wanted the job, and Washington was quick to appoint him. Congress wasn't in session to approve him, so he served in the interim. Then things went strangely awry. Rutledge made the mistake of criticizing the controversial Jay Treaty, a postwar agreement between the United States and Britain; many shared Rutledge's belief that the treaty was far too easy on the British. But given that his predecessor had negotiated the accord (and Washington had approved it), you'd think Rutledge would've been smart enough to keep his views to himself. He didn't, and his confirmation by Congress was not to be.

Toward the end of his life, Rutledge again served in the South Carolina legislature, but he was tragically deteriorating, both physically and mentally. His behavior became erratic, bizarre, and at times deranged. He twice attempted to drown himself. The second time, he waded fully clothed into Charleston's Ashley River, resisting and verbally abusing the men who came to his aid. Several factors contributed to his decline: the deaths of his wife and his younger brother Edward, a kidney ailment, and his inability to get his finances back on track. Creditors were closing in for the kill. The loss of love, money, health, and, arguably, position was a surefire recipe for a bad bout of depression.

Rutledge died at age sixty-one and is buried in St. Michael's Church in Charleston, the same churchyard that is the final resting place of his fellow signer Charles Cotesworth Pinckney. Today, you can visit his house and even spend the night there, amid the soaring palmetto trees and mint juleps. It is a lavishly ornate bed-and-breakfast in the historic district of Charleston.

★ ★ ★ ★ ★ ★ ★ ★ ★ ★ ★ ★

Charles Cotesworth Pinckney

★ ★ ★ ★ ★ ★ ★ ★ ★ ★ ★ ★

The Signer Who Wouldn't Bribe the French

BORN: February 25, 1746
DIED: August 16, 1825
AGE AT SIGNING: 41
PROFESSION: Lawyer, planter
BURIED: St. Michael's Church
    Cemetery, Charleston, South
    Carolina

★ ★ ★ ★ ★ ★ ★ ★ ★ ★ ★ ★

Oh, the French. America's relationship with the Gauls is a long, storied, and often contrary love affair. When France helped the colonies trounce the Crown, it appeared that *la vie* would be all *en rose* between the two nations. But after only a decade or so, the two countries were bickering, and war seemed imminent. Charles Cotesworth Pinckney earned a spot in the history books for escalating rather than defusing the tensions. In one notable encounter, he told the French to stick it.

Pinckney was the son of an extraordinary woman who single-handedly introduced to the colonies a miracle crop—indigo—that would eventually account for one-third of South Carolina's exports. This ancient plant produced a rich blue dye prized by textile manufacturers since antiquity. Once Pickney's mother shared its secrets with her planter neighbors, South Carolina was well on its way to one day becoming the wealthiest state in the union.

When Pinckney was only seven years old, his father (a judge) was assigned to serve as South Carolina's agent, or nonvoting representative, in Great Britain. Dad took the family to live with him in London. Though his parents returned home five years later, Charles Cotesworth stayed behind to study law at Oxford and Middle Temple. He finished with a tour of Germany and a stint at a French military school and then returned home to South Carolina to work for his colony's royal attorney general. And he married Sarah Middleton, whose father was the wealthiest planter in the colony.

South Carolina was one of the first colonies to declare itself independent from Mother England. Pinckney, who had already participated in patriotic assemblies, became a captain in the first South Carolina regiment. He defended his beloved city from a sea attack by the British in 1775, fought at Germantown and Brandywine in Pennsylvania, and led troops in a losing battle against British forces in Florida. When the Redcoats besieged Charleston in 1780, Pinckney was among the soldiers captured. Unlike his brothers-in-law (and Declaration of Independence signers) Edward Rutledge and Arthur Middleton, who were shipped off to serve time in St. Augustine, Florida, Pinckney was imprisoned just outside Charleston. When he fell ill, British officers allowed him to return home to recuperate as long as he (a) agreed not to take up arms and (b) remained confined to his property. Pinckney arrived home to learn two things: his only son had just died, and his parole had been revoked. Grieving and ill, he returned to prison until his release in February 1782. His wife, who was not yet thirty years old, died in 1784.

The war damaged Pinckney's finances, but, unlike many of the founding fathers, he managed to recover; he was dazzlingly wealthy to the end of his days. People said his law practice didn't bill clients who were widows, meaning that he was kind and charitable to damsels in distress, but the truth is that he didn't need the money. While some of the signers of the Constitution were raising families on incomes of a few hundred pounds a year, Pinckney was raking in more than four thousand! No wonder he's smiling in his most famous portrait.

In the spring of 1787, Pinckney arrived in Philadelphia with his new bride, Mary Stead, and soon became one of the more influential men at the Constitutional Convention. (Charles Pinckney, his second cousin, also attended.) He had an excellent grasp of law and wasn't afraid to speak up. As a man of his time, Pinckney believed that no senator should receive a salary, which would have ensured that only wealthy men would serve in that capacity. Moreover, he insisted on provisions in the document to protect religious freedom.

But Pinckney is best known as an unabashed defender of the southern way of life. If his southern compatriots were to support the Constitution, they had to be sure not to sign away their rights to a government that would later abolish slavery at will. That meant having a strong voice—and thus lots of representatives—in Congress. Pinckney thought that slaves should be counted 100 percent toward a state's total population. The larger a state's population, the more power it would wield in the new Congress. But nonslaveholding delegates saw this stance as hypocritical. Enslaved blacks were not free humans; they were property. Pinckney was willing to compromise on this point, if only someone would meet him and his fellow southern delegates halfway. In the end, of course, the Convention met them three-fifths of the way. Later, when the founders agreed not to interfere with the slave trade until 1800, Pinckney pressured them to adopt the later date of 1808. Doing so had profound consequences, since tens of thousands of new slaves were brought into the United States between 1800 and 1808.

After signing, Pinckney supported the Constitution and pushed South Carolina to become the eighth state to ratify. When asked why the Constitution lacked a Bill of Rights, the canny lawyer responded frankly, "Such bills generally begin with declaring that men are by nature born free. Now, we would make that declaration with very bad grace when a large part of our property consists in men who are actually born slaves."

President Washington thrice offered Pinckney powerful posts—he declined every time. Only an offer to return to France as his nation's envoy galvanized him. But when he crossed the pond with his family in late 1796, he received a snooty welcome from the French. Unfortunately, tensions had been building between the United States and its former ally; people feared war was imminent. His new hosts told Pinckney not to let the French doors hit him in the derrière on the way out of *la nation.* As soon as John Adams became president, he sent John Marshall and Elbridge Gerry—a signer of the Declaration of Independence—to help Pinckney smooth things over. The Americans were approached by a French trio who demanded bribes in exchange for brokering peace between the two nations. Furious, Pinckney exclaimed: "It is no, no! Not a sixpence!" The incident became known as the XYZ Affair.

Returning home in the fall of 1798, Pinckney was pressed into service in the new American army as the United States prepared for an inevitable war with France. Both Washington—now a former president—and Alexander Hamilton would lead troops, with Pinckney as their number three. But before anyone could rename their French fries, a fresh group of American envoys got a friendlier response from the French, and everything blew over as easily as a storm at sea.

Now a hero for his defiant rebuke of the French, Pinckney might have seemed like a smart pick as John Adams's running mate in the difficult 1800 election, but the pair lost to Thomas Jefferson and Aaron Burr. Adams quit politics forever, Hamilton took a bullet in a duel, and Pinckney was now heir apparent of the Federalist Party. He ran for president in 1804 and 1808, losing both times. He finally threw in the towel and retired to his estate on Pinckney Island, on the coast of South Carolina. Following in his mother's footsteps, he began experimenting with plants. A fellow botanist and friend named an attractive deciduous shrub found in the Southeast in his honor: the Pinckneya. Pinckney stayed active in his local community, even joining a group that distributed Bibles to slaves. When he died in 1825, at the age of seventy-nine, he was buried in the grave-yard of Charleston's prettiest church, in the shade of its gleaming white steeple.

* * * * * * * * * * * * *

Charles Pinckney

★ ★ ★ ★ ★ ★ ★ ★ ★ ★ ★ ★

The Ghost Writer of the Constitution?

BORN: October 26, 1757
DIED: October 29, 1824
AGE AT SIGNING: 29
PROFESSION: Lawyer
BURIED: St. Philip's Church,
      Charleston, South Carolina

★ ★ ★ ★ ★ ★ ★ ★ ★ ★ ★ ★

Young, active, and maybe a little too aggressive, Charles Pinckney was a man with a plan—the Pinckney Plan, that is. His proposal for the new government, presented at the Constitutional Convention, had been almost completely lost and forgotten until some twentieth-century sleuthing helped shed light on his contributions to the Constitution—and what some believe to be a possible smear job by James Madison.

Born in Charleston to a wealthy lawyer, planter, and militia colonel, Pinckney enjoyed the life of a privileged child of the coastal south. He had servants, tutors, books, and every conceivable advantage. After studying law, he was admitted to the bar and began his practice in Charleston. He decided to take up the political mantle but went in a much more revolutionary direction than his father, Charles Sr., who had been politically active, too, but was not a patriot.

Among the youngest signers, Pinckney came of age during the height of the Revolutionary War. In 1779, he was elected to the South Carolina legislature and joined the militia. He fought battles in Savannah and Charleston and was captured when the latter city fell to the British in 1780. He was released via a prisoner exchange in 1781.

At war's end, Pinckney worked on the state level and, later, was a delegate to the Congress of the Confederation, While there, he began expressing a desire to strengthen the national government, writing pamphlets explaining why the Articles of Confederation needed to be changed. In 1786, he served as a chairman on a congressional subcommittee tasked with drawing up some of the recommendations for amending the articles. With all that under his belt, it was little surprise then that in 1787, at the age of twenty-nine, Pinckney was sent to the Constitutional Convention.

Although still young, Pinckney was no wallflower at the big dance. He spoke forcefully and often—reportedly more than a hundred times. But he did more than just talk. An early advocate of changing the Articles of Confederation, he had done his homework and drawn up his own detailed plan for what the Constitution might look like.

And on May 29, according to James Madison's notes, Pinckney presented his plan. That's pretty much all Madison records. Curiously, he goes into no detail, nor does he describe the plan, which seems odd.

Consider that we know a great deal about the Virginia Plan, which was presented by Edmund Randolph. And that we have plenty of documentation regarding William Paterson's New Jersey Plan. Both proposals were extensively discussed and then passed on to the Committee of Detail, headed by John Rutledge, which considered them while creating the first draft of the Constitution. But to this day no copy exists of the mysterious Pinckney Plan, which explains why most Americans have never heard of Charles Pinckney.

Here's where the story gets tricky.

Later in Pinckney's life, then secretary of state John Quincy Adams was preparing to publish a journal about the Convention. In notes kept by convention secretary William Jackson, Adams had come across a reference to Pinckney's plan and wrote asking Pinckney to send him a copy. Pinckney obliged, saying that he had several different copies. He forwarded to Adams the version that he believed to be the one he had presented to Congress.

The plan was remarkably similar in content and language to the final Constitution.

When Madison got wind of this episode, he was none too pleased. He waited until after Pinckney had died—at least six years, possibly more—before he began raising suspicions about the veracity of the document sent to Adams. It was too similar to the final Constitution, he said. (Subtext: Pinckney faked it.) True, there was no love lost between Madison and Pinckney in life. Madison was modest; Pinckney had a tendency to lay on the charm and was not averse to bragging. Madison was shy and reserved; Pinckney was outspoken, in-your-face, and rumored to be popular with the ladies. In short, Madison was country, and Pinckney was rock 'n roll.

After both men were dead, scholars continued investigating the case of the missing plan. And a problem arose: the paper and ink of the version sent to Adams by Pinckney did not date from the time of the Convention. It appeared the document was misdated—and Pinckney was busted.

Until, that is, early in the twentieth century, when scholars reviewing the papers of James Wilson made a startling discovery. In his papers, Wilson describes Pinckney's plan, including an outline and extracts from it. Historians discovered that Pinckney's plan had been presented to the Convention not once but twice, yet the details never made it into Madison's copious notes. Why the omission? Defenders of Madison say he may have been out of the room. A less charitable view is that Madison was trying to ensure that Pinckney and his ideas were forgotten by history.

Over the years, countless scholars have tried to reconstruct the missing Pinckney Plan; some estimate that thirty to forty provisions in the Constitution came from Pinckney's suggestions. It's believed that he introduced the idea of calling the nation's leader "president," the first use of the words "House" and "Senate," and the idea of the president's annual State of the Union address.

Regardless of who contributed what, Pinckney signed the Constitution and worked to get it ratified in South Carolina. In 1788, he married Mary Eleanor Laurens, daughter of Henry Laurens, a former president of the Continental Congress and a very, very rich man. Pinckney was elected governor for the first of four times in 1789, headed up the convention that worked on a new constitution for South Carolina, and took office again in 1791.

He went to the state legislature in 1792 and abandoned the Federalists to become a Democratic-Republican (this metamorphosis was spurred along by President George Washington's approval of the Jay Treaty, which seemed to go soft on the nation's old enemy, Britain). In fact, Pinckney was so opposed to the treaty that he wanted Jay removed from his post as chief justice. Incensed that Pinckney would turn coat, his former Federalist buddies mocked him with the nickname "Blackguard Charlie." Despite the ribbing from his old pals, he again became his state's governor in 1796—the first Democratic-Republican to do so—and in 1798 was elected a senator.

During the heated election of 1800, Pinckney supported Jefferson, even though his cousin, Charles Cotesworth Pinckney, was John Adams's running mate. Jefferson won South Carolina's electoral votes, and our man Pinckney became minister to Spain. Though he didn't convince Spain to hand over Florida to the United States, he was considered instrumental in getting that country's cooperation during the Louisiana Purchase. After returning from Spain, he toggled between the South Carolina state house and the governorship. His last stint in public office was as a U.S. representative.

One of the last signers to die, Pinckney left this world at the age of sixty-seven. Today, one of his homes is a National Historic Site in Mount Pleasant, South Carolina, on Sullivan's Island, and is open to the public. The signer was originally buried at St. Philip's Church in Charleston, but the location of his grave remains as mysterious as that of the original draft of his infamous plan.

* * * * * * * * * * * * *

Pierce Butler

* * * * * * * * * * * *

The Signer Who Turned Coat on the King

BORN: July 11, 1744
DIED: February 15, 1822
AGE AT SIGNING: 43
PROFESSION: Soldier, planter
BURIED: Christ Church,
      Philadelphia, Pennsylvania

* * * * * * * * * * * *

When His Majesty's soldiers arrived in America in the mid- to late 1760s, they came to defend unpopular acts of Parliament and to quell civil unrest. Many were impressed with the lives of the colonists. From what they saw, Americans had it pretty good: Abundant land. Three square meals. Education for their children. Clear, running streams. Pleasant orchards. *Just what were they griping about? Try living in dark, crowded London for a change!*

Arriving in the aftermath of the Boston Massacre, one officer from the Crown's Twenty-ninth Regiment liked the colonies so much he decided to stay. That soldier, Pierce Butler, sold his position in the British army to another wealthy officer wannabe in 1773, only two years after Butler had married Mary Middleton of South Carolina.

He was the son of an Irish baronet who belonged to the very same Parliament that was so agitating the colonists. But young Butler probably felt he had nothing to lose by leaving his Boston post: as his father's third son, he would never inherit the family property and had been forced to enter the military at the age of eleven. Free from service, he used the cash from his commission to start an empire that included ten thousand acres of plantation in South Carolina and Georgia, plus a fleet of ships. When the Revolutionary War broke out, he worked in his state's militia against his king and former brothers in arms, pumping money and supplies into the patriot cause.

Like Charles Cotesworth Pinckney, Butler found himself on a hit list of British revolutionaries who saw their property and slaves confiscated. After the war, when the British military pulled out, Butler was left to rebuild his fortunes. He sailed to the Netherlands, hocked all his land to a Dutch firm, and received a sizable loan, which he used to buy a fresh batch of slaves and equipment. He thus adroitly sidestepped the high interest being charging by local banks at the end of the war, when everyone was trying to rebuild. Still, the Dutch loan, combined with a few bad rice harvests, nearly ruined him. The only reason his creditors didn't swoop in to seize his property was that South Carolina passed an emergency law in 1786 to prevent such actions. It also helped that he was then a member of the legislature that passed the ruling.

Butler arrived at the Constitutional Convention in 1787 a somewhat desperate man with shaky finances. But you wouldn't have known it from the gold-laced jacket he wore and the way he crowed about his blue-blood lineage. Yet, for all his pride, he worked diligently on behalf of a strong central government. It was he who suggested that the delegates keep all deliberations secret, a measure that the convention adopted wholeheartedly on day one. At first, Butler wasn't sure that Congress should abandon the Articles of Confederation, and he fought the Virginia Plan when it was presented in the early days of the convention. His argument was: *Are we really smart enough, capable enough, and experienced enough to try a form of government never used anywhere on the planet?* But as he listened to James Madison and the other delegates, he changed his mind. Others in attendance were moved by his example and did the same.

Butler spoke about seventy times during the proceedings, and not always with consistency. He's often remembered as defender of the "common man," because he charged that the delegates represented only the nation's elite. And he was right: there were few at the convention who represented the rights of the small tradesmen, farmers, and backwoods folks. But Butler later argued that allowing ordinary people to vote was impractical. He was hardly alone in this position. By serving on the committee that hammered out the details of the Electoral College—which some say was his idea—he and his fellow founders neatly inserted one more "check" between the top offices in the land and the voting public they often feared would be too ill informed to choose wisely.

Butler was sometimes full of contradictions. On one occasion, he said that no Congressman should ever take a salary; on another, he said they should be handsomely paid. He objected to allowing immigrants to sit on Congress, arguing that they were "dangerous," although he himself was an immigrant, a fact that was not lost on him. Indeed, he admitted that he would've made a lousy politician had he been allowed to serve soon after arriving on colonial shores. But he is probably best known as the man responsible for the Constitution's fugitive slave clause, which states that slaves who fled to other states could be returned to their masters.

After the convention, Butler supported the Constitution but didn't attend the South Carolina convention where the document was ratified. He served as a U.S. senator for three terms and was on the short list to run for his state's governorship, though he never did. He was not in love with politics and thought it brought out the worst in men. "I am materially disappointed," he wrote to a friend. "I find men scrambling for partial advantages, State interests, and in short, a train of those narrow, impolitic measures that must, after a while, shake the Union to its very foundation." Accordingly, he was always an independent in his politics. He switched parties three times and, even then, still often opposed his allies of-the-moment.

The years immediately after the convention brought Butler good luck and a bountiful harvest, and by 1790 his finances were healthy. Soon he had five hundred slaves working eleven hundred acres in South Carolina and Georgia. By this point he was one of the richest men in America, and he kicked back and watched the checks roll in. He bought homes in Philadelphia and moved there to be with a daughter. He supported slavery, the backbone of his wealth, till the end of his days.

Considering how he'd been maltreated by family inheritance, you'd think Butler would've been kind to his own progeny. But no. Instead, he became an odd and controlling old gent. He cut some of his children out of his will and promised to reward a son-in-law who named his own son Pierce Butler. That grandson married a British actress who was so horrified by the slavery practices she witnessed that she filed for divorce and published a tell-all book about her horrific experience in Georgia. Her husband squandered his fortune and was forced to sell his slaves in what was the largest human auction in U.S. history.

Upon his death in 1822, at age seventy-seven, Butler was buried just outside the walls of Christ Church in Philadelphia. And thus the soldier who liked America so much settled in for the long haul.

★ ★ ★ ★ ★ ★ ★ ★ ★ ★ ★ ★

XII. Georgia

William Few

The Signer Who Lived the American Dream

BORN: June 8, 1748
DIED: July 16, 1828
AGE AT SIGNING: 39
PROFESSION: Farmer, lawyer
BURIED: St. Paul's Episcopal
Church, Augusta, Georgia

★ ★ ★ ★ ★ ★ ★ ★ ★ ★ ★

An undereducated frontier farm boy who went on to become a lawyer and a signer of the Constitution, William Few—perhaps more than any of the other signers—best exemplified the American Dream, and that at a time when America was just getting started.

Born on a family farm in Baltimore County, Maryland, Few came from humble beginnings. His father was a Quaker farmer, his mother a Catholic; later, Few would align himself with the Methodist faith. He received little proper schooling and certainly no money to send him off to be educated, as other prosperous planters often did for their children. He once described an early experience at a country school as being fraught with "terror and anxiety," primarily because of a teacher he abhorred.

When Few was about ten years old, the family moved to North Carolina in hopes of finding better weather and, with it, more productive crops. The life of a frontier farmer was a difficult one, and Few, like many young men, soon found himself learning to work the land. His second year of schooling was his last and, by his own account, very enjoyable. He was just twelve years old, but the schoolmaster-for-hire with whom he studied was to his liking. This relationship gave Few a love of reading and learning that would shape the rest of his life.

At age sixteen, Few and his family moved again, this time to the small town of Hillsborough. By then, Few was teaching himself, reading every book he could get his hands on and visiting the courthouse to listen to arguments. When he was nineteen years old, his father gave him his own plot of land to work. Even then, he took a book with him when it was time to plow, occasionally taking a break to read during the long days in the fields.

The North Carolina frontier became a hotbed of revolution that preceded the war against the British. The Regulator movement was taking hold, pitting farmers against landed gentry or other gentlemen of the seaboard who were viewed as privileged folk in control of all the state's money and power. Their appointees were corrupt officials and sheriffs who took advantage of the working man at every turn. Few's family was caught up in the class struggle. The height of the rebellion was the battle of Alamance, where Governor William Tryon, leading the colonial militia, crushed the uprising. Few's brother was captured and hanged for his part in the fighting. The family farm was destroyed and Few's father, besieged by creditors, eventually fled to Georgia; Few stayed behind to clean up his family's affairs, providing the young man with even more experience—some of it less than pleasant—with courts and lawyers.

As the Revolutionary War approached, farmers and gentry alike were beginning to unify against the British. Few jumped on the militia bandwagon in Hillsborough and helped form a volunteer company. He attended meetings to understand the nature of the conflict. "I felt the spirit of an American," he wrote, "and without much investigation of the justice of her cause, I resolved to defend it."

He joined his family near Augusta, Georgia, and quickly became known in both business and the patriotic movement. He continued fighting with the militia forces there, eventually earning the rank of lieutenant colonel. His political life began in 1777, when he was elected to the convention in Savannah that created the Georgia constitution. He was appointed to the state's first legislature, served on the governor's advisory council, and eventually worked as surveyor general of the state, commissioner of confiscated estates, and senior justice for Richmond County.

Few also saw fighting in the American Revolution. In 1778, he and his militia brothers fended off British forces on the state's southeast border as well as in Florida, a trip that proved disastrous for the troops, many of whom fell sick in the swamps. On December 28, 1778, the British took Savannah, then the colony's capital. In 1780, he was elected to attend Congress (at that time still based in Philadelphia); when he returned to Georgia, he served in the state legislature and focused on his law practice. All his reading and careful attention to court cases paid off; the self-taught lawyer built a successful practice in Augusta. He later wrote that he had "never spent one hour in the office of an attorney to prepare for the business, nor did I know anything of the practice."

In 1786, Few returned to Congress, which by that time had relocated to New York City. The next year he was sent to the Constitutional Convention in Philadelphia, and so shuttled back and forth between the two cities. Given the circumstances, his attendance was surprisingly steady. He was one of the rare signers who hailed from the farming class—small, subsistence, plow-your-own-fields farming. Of him fellow Georgia delegate William Pierce wrote: "Mr. Few possesses a strong natural Genius, and from application has acquired some knowledge of legal matters; —he practices at the bar of Georgia, and speaks tolerably well in the Legislature. He has been twice a

Member of Congress, and served in that capacity with fidelity to his State, and honor to himself."

He signed, he ratified, and he served as one of his state's first senators. His travels to Congress in New York City brought him more than political clout, it brought him personal satisfaction, too: in 1788, he married Catherine Nicholson, a New Yorker. During his term as senator, Few witnessed George Washington being sworn in as president. But over time, he found himself increasingly drawn to the views of Thomas Jefferson and opposed to Alexander Hamilton's fiscal policies.

Upon leaving the Senate in 1793, Few moved with his wife to Columbia County, Georgia. He ran for the Senate again in 1796, but lost. He served as a judge for three years before deciding to shake things up and move back to New York City. The relocation may have been because of his wife's homesickness, but Few did write about the "scorching climate of Georgia" and "accumulating evils of fevers and Negro slavery," which he regarded as "enemies to humane felicity." He and Catherine were Big Apple–bound.

Few's resume carried weight in that city as well, and the end of his life was peppered with a variety of appointments and official posts. In 1801, he was elected to the New York legislature, where he served three years. He served as inspector of the state prisons for a decade, a state commissioner of loans, director of Manhattan Bank, president of City Bank, and a city alderman to boot.

When Few finally retired to his country home in Dutchess County at the age of sixty-eight, he estimated his wealth to be worth more than $100,000—not bad for a frontier farm boy born into poverty and deprived of a formal education. He died at the respectable age of eighty at the home of his daughter, in what was then Fishkill-on-Hudson (now Beacon), New York. He was originally buried at the Reformed Dutch Church, but his body was later moved—everybody loves to dig up the signers—to St. Paul's Church in Augusta, Georgia.

Abr Baldwin

★ ★ ★ ★ ★ ★ ★ ★ ★ ★ ★ ★

The Signer Who Pinched Pennies

BORN: November 22, 1754

DIED: March 4, 1807

AGE AT SIGNING: 32

PROFESSION: Chaplain, lawyer, politician

BURIED: Rock Creek Cemetery, Washington, D.C.

★ ★ ★ ★ ★ ★ ★ ★ ★ ★ ★ ★

Abraham Baldwin, a mousy chaplain-turned-lawyer, was the chief actor in the most dramatic moment of the Constitutional Convention. Though he'd gone to Philadelphia on behalf of Georgia, he was a born-and-bred Connecticut Yankee. But when his big moment arrived, he managed to set aside all of his allegiances and act for the good of the nation.

To most other delegates, the state of Georgia was something of a mystery. It was sizable enough on a map, but it was populated sparsely with only 25,000 people, most of them settled at the prosperous coast. By rights, Georgia should have been voting en bloc with the small states on the important but divisive issue of congressional representation. But, from day one at the convention, Georgia and the other "small" southern states—North Carolina,

South Carolina, and Maryland—debated as though they had a large population the size of, say, Virginia's. They couldn't make that claim just yet, but they certainly had plenty of room to grow.

And new citizens were arriving every day. Then, as now, people moved in droves to the Sun Belt in search of better climates and opportunities. When the Declaration of Independence was signed, none of the Georgia delegates had been born in Georgia. Eleven years later, none of the men representing Georgia at the Constitutional Convention had been born there, either, including Abraham Baldwin.

Baldwin was the son of an ambitious Connecticut blacksmith and widower who was willing to sink heavily into debt to ensure that his twelve children received a good education. At age thirteen, Abraham, the second son, went to Yale to study theology and, after graduating in 1772, stayed on there to tutor other students. When the Revolutionary War broke out, he endured a miserable winter preaching the gospel to Washington's troops, who were encamped at Morristown, New Jersey. In his spare time, he read law books. When his serviced ended, Baldwin's life was at a crossroads. Yale offered him a high-paying job as a professor of theology, but he turned it down, choosing law instead. He practiced a year in Connecticut but felt dissatisfied, stifled. The little state was bursting with lawyers, many better trained than he.

So Baldwin headed south to Georgia, settling in the rural backwoods near Augusta, where he bonded with the locals. As his father had been, Baldwin's new neighbors were self-reliant tradesmen and farmers who didn't have much money. Some of them may have owned a few slaves, but they shared little in common with the flashy owners of the vast plantations near Savannah. Baldwin was elected to the state legislature only three months after arriving in Augusta and, soon after, was chosen for Congress. By the time he was sent to the Constitutional Convention, he'd been a full-fledged Georgia resident for a mere three years.

Baldwin had no farm or business investments. He did not dabble in land speculation. There was no inheritance waiting for him. (In fact, when his father died, there were only more debts to be paid.) His law practice did fine, but his most regular income seems to have come from jobs in Congress and the state. Since he had so little money, we can only assume that Baldwin lived rather frugally. It probably helped that he had no family of his own to support. He became known for mentoring young men, paying for their schooling and helping them get a start in business. At age thirty-two, he was one of the convention's three bachelors, along with Nicholas Gilman of New Hampshire and Daniel of St. Thomas Jenifer of Maryland.

As a delegate, Baldwin spoke only a few times, but he was chosen for all the important committees. His big moment came after it had been agreed that the number of congressmen in the House would be determined by the population of each state. With that decided, the small states demanded equal representation in the Senate. Every time the topic was discussed, the big states appeared to have more votes. On June 30, Delaware's Gunning Bedford angrily denounced his colleagues from the more-populous states. The conventioneers adjourned for a Sunday cool-down. When they returned on Monday, July 2, the entire body took a vote: *Should the Senate have equal suffrage?*

Down the list of delegates they went, voting north to south. In the end, the decision fell to Baldwin, the last man to cast a vote. In the past, he'd been pushed around by his three fellow Georgia delegates, who always sided with the big states. But two of those men, convention scribe William Pierce and Methodist William Few, were absent, having left to deal with congressional business in New York.

Georgia delegate and aristocrat William Houstoun voted no, in support of the big states. Then all eyes turned to Baldwin, a man who pinched pennies and managed to pay off his dead father's debts and send his siblings to school on an income of only $9 a day; a man who had little in common with the fat-cat planters; a man who saw his constituents as the equals of his Yankee forbears; a man who knew that underpopulated, vulnerable Georgia desperately needed

Signing Their Rights Away

the protection of a strong government.

Baldwin voted *yes*.

Georgia was tied, and thus voided. For the first time, the votes of the big and the small states were even, and thus the two sides were *equal* in the eyes of the convention.

It was as if the scales had fallen from everyone's eyes. The delegates now realized that, for the sake of the union, they *had* to compromise. The small states must have their way on something, or there would be no true United States of America. The deadlock was finally broken.

After the convention, Baldwin served as his state's representative to Congress. His levelheadedness was prized, and in 1788 he was asked to help James Madison draw up the Bill of Rights in committee. His voters sent him to the U.S. Senate twice, in 1798 and 1804, but he didn't live to finish his second term. Struck down by an unknown illness, he lay dying in a bed at his sister's house in Washington, D.C., while friends and family fussed over him. Though sick, he enjoyed telling them how, until then, he'd never missed a day in Congress. On the eighth day, he died; he was only fifty-three years old. Baldwin was buried first on the grounds of his sister's estate, but his body was later moved to a cemetery in downtown Washington, D.C.

A strong proponent of education, he is fondly remembered by Georgians for creating what would later become the University of Georgia, the first such school chartered by a state.

* * * * * * * * * * * *

Appendix I.

Text of the U.S. Constitution

★ ★

We the People of the United States, in Order to form a more perfect Union, establish Justice, insure domestic Tranquility, provide for the common defence, promote the general Welfare, and secure the Blessings of Liberty to ourselves and our Posterity, do ordain and establish this Constitution for the United States of America.

Article 1.

Section 1

All legislative Powers herein granted shall be vested in a Congress of the United States, which shall consist of a Senate and House of Representatives.

Section 2

The House of Representatives shall be composed of Members chosen every second Year by the People of the several States, and the Electors in each State shall have the Qualifications requisite for Electors of the most numerous Branch of the State Legislature.

No Person shall be a Representative who shall not have attained to the Age of twenty five Years, and been seven Years a Citizen of the United States, and who shall not, when elected, be an Inhabitant of that State in which he shall be chosen.

Representatives and direct Taxes shall be apportioned among the several States which may be included within this Union, according to their respective Numbers, which shall be determined by adding to the whole Number of free Persons, including those bound to Service for a Term of Years, and excluding Indians not taxed, three fifths of all other Persons. The actual Enumeration shall be made within three Years after the first Meeting of the Congress of the United States, and within every subsequent Term of ten Years, in such Manner as they shall by Law direct. The Number of Representatives shall not exceed one for every thirty Thousand, but each State shall have at Least one Representative; and until such enumeration shall be made, the State of New Hampshire shall be entitled to choose three, Massachusetts eight, Rhode Island and Providence Plantations one, Connecticut five, New York six, New Jersey four, Pennsylvania eight, Delaware one, Maryland six, Virginia ten, North Carolina five, South Carolina five and Georgia three.

When vacancies happen in the Representation from any State, the

Signing Their Rights Away

Executive Authority thereof shall issue Writs of Election to fill such Vacancies.

The House of Representatives shall chuse their Speaker and other Officers; and shall have the sole Power of Impeachment.

Section 3

The Senate of the United States shall be composed of two Senators from each State, chosen by the Legislature thereof, for six Years; and each Senator shall have one Vote.

Immediately after they shall be assembled in Consequence of the first Election, they shall be divided as equally as may be into three Classes. The Seats of the Senators of the first Class shall be vacated at the Expiration of the second Year, of the second Class at the Expiration of the fourth Year, and of the third Class at the Expiration of the sixth Year, so that one third may be chosen every second Year; and if Vacancies happen by Resignation, or otherwise, during the Recess of the Legislature of any State, the Executive thereof may make temporary Appointments until the next Meeting of the Legislature, which shall then fill such Vacancies.

No person shall be a Senator who shall not have attained to the Age of thirty Years, and been nine Years a Citizen of the United States, and who shall not,

when elected, be an Inhabitant of that State for which he shall be chosen.

The Vice President of the United States shall be President of the Senate, but shall have no Vote, unless they be equally divided.

The Senate shall chuse their other Officers, and also a President pro tempore, in the absence of the Vice President, or when he shall exercise the Office of President of the United States.

The Senate shall have the sole Power to try all Impeachments. When sitting for that Purpose, they shall be on Oath or Affirmation. When the President of the United States is tried, the Chief Justice shall preside: And no Person shall be convicted without the Concurrence of two thirds of the Members present.

Judgment in Cases of Impeachment shall not extend further than to removal from Office, and disqualification to hold and enjoy any Office of honor, Trust or Profit under the United States: but the Party convicted shall nevertheless be liable and subject to Indictment, Trial, Judgment and Punishment, according to Law.

Section 4

The Times, Places and Manner of holding Elections for Senators and Representatives, shall be prescribed in each State by the Legislature thereof; but the Congress may at any time by Law make or alter such Regulations, except as to the Places of Chusing Senators.

The Congress shall assemble at least once in every Year, and such Meeting shall be on the first Monday in December, unless they shall by Law appoint a different Day.

Section 5

Each House shall be the Judge of the Elections, Returns and Qualifications of its own Members, and a Majority of each shall constitute a Quorum to do Business; but a smaller number may adjourn from day to day, and may be authorized to compel the Attendance of absent Members, in such Manner, and under such Penalties as each House may provide.

Each House may determine the Rules of its Proceedings, punish its Members for disorderly Behavior, and, with the Concurrence of two thirds, expel a Member.

Each House shall keep a Journal of its Proceedings, and from time to time publish the same, excepting such Parts as may in their Judgment require Secrecy; and the Yeas and Nays of the Members of either House on any question shall, at the Desire of one fifth of those Present, be entered on the Journal.

Neither House, during the Session of Congress, shall, without the Consent of the other, adjourn for more than three days, nor to any other Place than that in which the two Houses shall be sitting.

Section 6

The Senators and Representatives shall receive a Compensation for their Services, to be ascertained by Law, and paid out of the Treasury of the United States. They shall in all Cases, except Treason, Felony and Breach of the Peace, be privileged from Arrest during their Attendance at the Session of their respective Houses, and in going to and returning from the same; and for any Speech or Debate in either House, they shall not be questioned in any other Place.

No Senator or Representative shall, during the Time for which he was elected, be appointed to any civil Office under the Authority of the United States, which shall have been created, or the Emoluments whereof shall have been encreased during such time; and no Person holding any Office under the United States, shall be a Member of either House during his Continuance in Office.

Section 7

All bills for raising Revenue shall originate in the House of Representatives; but the Senate may propose or concur with Amendments as on other Bills.

Every Bill which shall have passed the House of Representatives and the Senate, shall, before it become a Law, be presented to the President of the United States; If he approve he shall sign it, but if not he shall return it, with his Objections to that House in which it shall have originated, who shall enter the Objections at large on their Journal, and proceed to reconsider it. If after such Reconsideration two thirds of that House shall agree to pass the Bill, it shall be sent, together with the Objections, to the other House, by which it shall likewise be reconsidered, and if approved by two thirds of that House, it shall become a Law. But in all such Cases the Votes of both Houses shall be determined by Yeas and Nays, and the Names of the Persons voting for and against the Bill shall be entered on the Journal of each House respectively. If any Bill shall not be returned by the President within ten Days (Sundays excepted) after it shall have been presented to him, the Same shall be a Law, in like Manner as if he had signed it, unless the Congress by their Adjournment prevent its Return, in which Case it shall not be a Law.

Every Order, Resolution, or Vote to which the Concurrence of the Senate and House of Representatives may be necessary (except on a question of Adjournment) shall be presented to the President of the United States; and before the Same shall take Effect, shall be approved by him, or being disapproved by him, shall be repassed by two thirds of the Senate and House of Representatives, according to the Rules and Limitations prescribed in the Case of a Bill.

Section 8

The Congress shall have Power To lay and collect Taxes, Duties, Imposts and Excises, to pay the Debts and provide for the common Defence and general Welfare of the United States; but all Duties, Imposts and Excises shall be uniform throughout the United States;

To borrow money on the credit of the United States;

To regulate Commerce with foreign Nations, and among the several States, and with the Indian Tribes;

To establish an uniform Rule of Naturalization, and uniform Laws on the subject of Bankruptcies throughout the United States;

To coin Money, regulate the Value thereof, and of foreign Coin, and fix the Standard of Weights and Measures;

To provide for the Punishment of counterfeiting the Securities and current Coin of the United States;

To establish Post Offices and post Roads;

To promote the Progress of Science and useful Arts, by securing for limited Times to Authors and Inventors the exclusive Right to their respective Writings and Discoveries;

To constitute Tribunals inferior to the supreme Court;

To define and punish Piracies and Felonies committed on the high Seas, and Offenses against the Law of Nations;

To declare War, grant Letters of Marque and Reprisal, and make Rules concerning Captures on Land and Water;

To raise and support Armies, but no Appropriation of Money to that Use shall be for a longer Term than two Years;

To provide and maintain a Navy; To make Rules for the Government and Regulation of the land and naval Forces;

To provide for calling forth the Militia to execute the Laws of the Union, suppress Insurrections and repel Invasions;

To provide for organizing, arming, and disciplining, the Militia, and for governing such Part of them as may be employed in the Service of the United States, reserving to the States respectively, the Appointment of the Officers, and the Authority of training the Militia according to the discipline prescribed by Congress;

To exercise exclusive Legislation in all Cases whatsoever, over such District (not exceeding ten Miles square) as may, by Cession of particular States, and the acceptance of Congress, become the Seat of the Government of the United States, and to exercise like Authority over all Places purchased by the Consent of the Legislature of the State in which the Same shall be, for the Erection of Forts, Magazines, Arsenals, dock-Yards, and other needful Buildings; And

To make all Laws which shall be necessary and proper for carrying into Execution the foregoing Powers, and all other Powers vested by this Constitution in the Government of the United States, or in any Department or Officer thereof.

Section 9

The Migration or Importation of such Persons as any of the States now existing shall think proper to admit, shall not be prohibited by the Congress prior to the Year one thousand eight hundred and eight, but a Tax or duty may be imposed on such Importation, not exceeding ten dollars for each Person.

The privilege of the Writ of Habeas Corpus shall not be suspended, unless when in Cases of Rebellion or Invasion the public Safety may require it.

No Bill of Attainder or ex post facto Law shall be passed.

No Capitation, or other direct, Tax shall be laid, unless in Proportion to the Census or Enumeration herein before directed to be taken.

No Tax or Duty shall be laid on Articles exported from any State.

No Preference shall be given by any Regulation of Commerce or Revenue to the Ports of one State over those of another: nor shall Vessels bound to, or from, one State, be obliged to enter, clear, or pay Duties in another.

No Money shall be drawn from the Treasury, but in Consequence of Appropriations made by Law; and a regular Statement and Account of the Receipts and Expenditures of all public Money shall be published from time to time.

No Title of Nobility shall be granted by the United States: And no Person holding any Office of Profit or Trust under them, shall, without the Consent of the Congress, accept of any present, Emolument, Office, or Title, of any kind whatever, from any King, Prince or foreign State.

Section 10
No State shall enter into any Treaty, Alliance, or Confederation; grant Letters of Marque and Reprisal; coin Money; emit Bills of Credit; make any Thing but gold and silver Coin a Tender in Payment of Debts; pass any Bill of Attainder, ex post facto Law, or Law impairing the Obligation of Contracts, or grant any Title of Nobility.

No State shall, without the Consent of the Congress, lay any Imposts or Duties on Imports or Exports, except what may be absolutely necessary for executing its inspection Laws: and the net Produce of all Duties and Imposts, laid by any State on Imports or Exports, shall be for the Use of the Treasury of the United States; and all such Laws shall be subject to the Revision and Control of the Congress.

No State shall, without the Consent of Congress, lay any duty of Tonnage, keep Troops, or Ships of War in time of Peace, enter into any Agreement or Compact with another State, or with a foreign Power, or engage in War, unless actually invaded, or in such imminent Danger as will not admit of delay.

Article 2.
Section 1
The executive Power shall be vested in a President of the United States of America. He shall hold his Office during the Term of four Years, and, together with the Vice-President chosen for the same Term, be elected, as follows:

Each State shall appoint, in such Manner as the Legislature thereof may direct, a Number of Electors, equal to the whole Number of Senators and Representatives to which the State may be entitled in the Congress: but no Senator or Representative, or Person holding an Office of Trust or Profit under the United States, shall be appointed an Elector.

The Electors shall meet in their respective States, and vote by Ballot for two persons, of whom one at least shall not lie an Inhabitant of the same State with themselves. And they shall make a List of all the Persons voted for, and of the Number of Votes for each; which List they shall sign and certify, and transmit sealed to the Seat of the Government of the United States, directed to the President of the Senate. The President of the Senate shall, in the Presence of the Senate and House of Representatives, open all the Certificates, and the Votes shall then be counted. The Person having the greatest Number of Votes shall be the President, if such Number be a Majority of the whole Number of Electors appointed; and if there be more than one who have such Majority, and have an equal Number of Votes, then the House of Representatives shall immediately chuse by Ballot one of them for President; and if no Person have a Majority, then from the five highest on the List the said House shall in like

Manner chuse the President. But in chusing the President, the Votes shall be taken by States, the Representation from each State having one Vote; a quorum for this Purpose shall consist of a Member or Members from two-thirds of the States, and a Majority of all the States shall be necessary to a Choice. In every Case, after the Choice of the President, the Person having the greatest Number of Votes of the Electors shall be the Vice President. But if there should remain two or more who have equal Votes, the Senate shall chuse from them by Ballot the Vice-President.

The Congress may determine the Time of choosing the Electors, and the Day on which they shall give their Votes; which Day shall be the same throughout the United States.

No person except a natural born Citizen, or a Citizen of the United States, at the time of the Adoption of this Constitution, shall be eligible to the Office of President; neither shall any Person be eligible to that Office who shall not have attained to the Age of thirty-five Years, and been fourteen Years a Resident within the United States.

In Case of the Removal of the President from Office, or of his Death, Resignation, or Inability to discharge the Powers and Duties of the said Office,

Signing Their Rights Away

the same shall devolve on the Vice President, and the Congress may by Law provide for the Case of Removal, Death, Resignation or Inability, both of the President and Vice President, declaring what Officer shall then act as President, and such Officer shall act accordingly, until the Disability be removed, or a President shall be elected.

The President shall, at stated Times, receive for his Services, a Compensation, which shall neither be increased nor diminished during the Period for which he shall have been elected, and he shall not receive within that Period any other Emolument from the United States, or any of them.

Before he enter on the Execution of his Office, he shall take the following Oath or Affirmation: "I do solemnly swear (or affirm) that I will faithfully execute the Office of President of the United States, and will to the best of my Ability, preserve, protect and defend the Constitution of the United States."

Section 2

The President shall be Commander in Chief of the Army and Navy of the United States, and of the Militia of the several States, when called into the actual Service of the United States; he may require the Opinion, in writing, of the principal Officer in each of the executive Departments, upon any subject relating to the Duties of their respective Offices, and he shall have Power to Grant Reprieves and Pardons for Offenses against the United States, except in Cases of Impeachment.

He shall have Power, by and with the Advice and Consent of the Senate, to make Treaties, provided two thirds of the Senators present concur; and he shall nominate, and by and with the Advice and Consent of the Senate, shall appoint Ambassadors, other public Ministers and Consuls, Judges of the supreme Court, and all other Officers of the United States, whose Appointments are not herein otherwise provided for, and which shall be established by Law: but the Congress may by Law vest the Appointment of such inferior Officers, as they think proper, in the President alone, in the Courts of Law, or in the Heads of Departments.

The President shall have Power to fill up all Vacancies that may happen during the Recess of the Senate, by granting Commissions which shall expire at the End of their next Session.

Section 3

He shall from time to time give to the Congress Information of the State of the Union, and recommend to their Consideration such Measures as he shall judge necessary and expedient; he may, on extraordinary Occasions, convene both Houses, or either of them, and in Case of Disagreement between them, with Respect to the Time of Adjournment, he may adjourn them to such Time as he shall think proper; he shall receive Ambassadors and other public Ministers; he shall take Care that the Laws be faithfully executed, and shall Commission all the Officers of the United States.

Section 4
The President, Vice President and all civil Officers of the United States, shall be removed from Office on Impeachment for, and Conviction of, Treason, Bribery, or other high Crimes and Misdemeanors.

Article 3.
Section 1
The judicial Power of the United States, shall be vested in one supreme Court, and in such inferior Courts as the Congress may from time to time ordain and establish. The Judges, both of the supreme and inferior Courts, shall hold their Offices during good Behavior, and shall, at stated Times, receive for their Services, a Compensation, which shall not be diminished during their Continuance in Office.

Section 2
The judicial Power shall extend to all Cases, in Law and Equity, arising under this Constitution, the Laws of the United States, and Treaties made, or which shall be made, under their

Authority; to all Cases affecting Ambassadors, other public Ministers and Consuls; to all Cases of admiralty and maritime Jurisdiction; to Controversies to which the United States shall be a Party; to Controversies between two or more States; between a State and Citizens of another State; between Citizens of different States; between Citizens of the same State claiming Lands under Grants of different States, and between a State, or the Citizens thereof, and foreign States, Citizens or Subjects.

In all Cases affecting Ambassadors, other public Ministers and Consuls, and those in which a State shall be Party, the supreme Court shall have original Jurisdiction. In all the other Cases before mentioned, the supreme Court shall have appellate Jurisdiction, both as to Law and Fact, with such Exceptions, and under such Regulations as the Congress shall make.

The Trial of all Crimes, except in Cases of Impeachment, shall be by Jury; and such Trial shall be held in the State where the said Crimes shall have been committed; but when not committed within any State, the Trial shall be at such Place or Places as the Congress may by Law have directed.

Section 3
Treason against the United States, shall consist only in levying War

Signing Their Rights Away

against them, or in adhering to their Enemies, giving them Aid and Comfort. No Person shall be convicted of Treason unless on the Testimony of two Witnesses to the same overt Act, or on Confession in open Court.

The Congress shall have Power to declare the Punishment of Treason, but no Attainder of Treason shall work Corruption of Blood, or Forfeiture except during the Life of the Person attainted.

Article 4.
Section 1
Full Faith and Credit shall be given in each State to the public Acts, Records, and judicial Proceedings of every other State. And the Congress may by general Laws prescribe the Manner in which such Acts, Records and Proceedings shall be proved, and the Effect thereof.

Section 2
The Citizens of each State shall be entitled to al l Privileges and Immunities of Citizens in the several States.

A Person charged in any State with Treason, Felony, or other Crime, who shall flee from Justice, and be found in another State, shall on demand of the executive Authority of the State from which he fled, be delivered up, to be removed to the State having Jurisdiction of the Crime.

No Person held to Service or Labour in one State, under the Laws thereof, escaping into another, shall, in Consequence of any Law or Regulation therein, be discharged from such Service or Labour, but shall be delivered up on Claim of the Party to whom such Service or Labour may be due.

Section 3
New States may be admitted by the Congress into this Union; but no new States shall be formed or erected within the Jurisdiction of any other State; nor any State be formed by the Junction of two or more States, or parts of States, without the Consent of the Legislatures of the States concerned as well as of the Congress.

The Congress shall have Power to dispose of and make all needful Rules and Regulations respecting the Territory or other Property belonging to the United States; and nothing in this Constitution shall be so construed as to Prejudice any Claims of the United States, or of any particular State.

Section 4
The United States shall guarantee to every State in this Union a Republican Form of Government, and shall protect each of them against Invasion; and on Application of the Legislature, or of the Executive (when the Legislature cannot be convened) against domestic Violence.

Article 5.

The Congress, whenever two thirds of both Houses shall deem it necessary, shall propose Amendments to this Constitution, or, on the Application of the Legislatures of two thirds of the several States, shall call a Convention for proposing Amendments, which, in either Case, shall be valid to all Intents and Purposes, as Part of this Constitution, when ratified by the Legislatures of three fourths of the several States, or by Conventions in three fourths thereof, as the one or the other Mode of Ratification may be proposed by the Congress; Provided that no Amendment which may be made prior to the Year One thousand eight hundred and eight shall in any Manner affect the first and fourth Clauses in the Ninth Section of the first Article; and that no State, without its Consent, shall be deprived of its equal Suffrage in the Senate.

Article 6.

All Debts contracted and Engagements entered into, before the Adoption of this Constitution, shall be as valid against the United States under this Constitution, as under the Confederation.

This Constitution, and the Laws of the United States which shall be made in Pursuance thereof; and all Treaties made, or which shall be made, under the Authority of the United States, shall be the supreme Law of the Land; and the Judges in every State shall be bound thereby, any Thing in the Constitution or Laws of any State to the Contrary notwithstanding.

The Senators and Representatives before mentioned, and the Members of the several State Legislatures, and all executive and judicial Officers, both of the United States and of the several States, shall be bound by Oath or Affirmation, to support this Constitution; but no religious Test shall ever be required as a Qualification to any Office or public Trust under the United States.

Article 7.

The Ratification of the Conventions of nine States, shall be sufficient for the Establishment of this Constitution between the States so ratifying the Same.

Done in Convention by the Unanimous Consent of the States present the Seventeenth Day of September in the Year of our Lord one thousand seven hundred and Eighty seven and of the Independence of the United States of America the Twelfth In Witness whereof We have hereunto subscribed our Names,

[Signatures]

Text of the Bill of Rights

★ ★

Amendment 1

Congress shall make no law respecting an establishment of religion, or prohibiting the free exercise thereof; or abridging the freedom of speech, or of the press; or the right of the people peaceably to assemble, and to petition the Government for a redress of grievances.

Amendment 2

A well regulated Militia, being necessary to the security of a free State, the right of the people to keep and bear Arms, shall not be infringed.

Amendment 3

No Soldier shall, in time of peace be quartered in any house, without the consent of the Owner, nor in time of war, but in a manner to be prescribed by law.

Amendment 4

The right of the people to be secure in their persons, houses, papers, and effects, against unreasonable searches and seizures, shall not be violated, and no Warrants shall issue, but upon probable cause, supported by Oath or affirmation, and particularly describing the place to be searched, and the persons or things to be seized.

Amendment 5

No person shall be held to answer for a capital, or otherwise infamous crime, unless on a presentment or indictment of a Grand Jury, except in cases arising in the land or naval forces, or in the Militia, when in actual service in time of War or public danger; nor shall any person be subject for the same offense to be twice put in jeopardy of life or limb; nor shall be compelled in any criminal case to be a witness against himself, nor be deprived of life, liberty, or property, without due process of law; nor shall private property be taken for public use, without just compensation.

Amendment 6

In all criminal prosecutions, the accused shall enjoy the right to a speedy and public trial, by an impartial jury of the State and district wherein the crime shall have been committed, which district shall have been previously ascertained by law, and to be informed of the nature and cause of the accusation; to be confronted with the witnesses against him; to have compulsory process for obtaining witnesses in his favor, and to have the Assistance of Counsel for his defence.

Amendment 7

In Suits at common law, where the value in controversy shall exceed twenty dollars, the right of trial by jury shall be preserved, and no fact tried by a jury, shall be otherwise re-examined in any Court of the United States, than according to the rules of the common law.

Amendment 8

Excessive bail shall not be required, nor excessive fines imposed, nor cruel and unusual punishments inflicted.

Amendment 9

The enumeration in the Constitution, of certain rights, shall not be construed to deny or disparage others retained by the people.

Amendment 10

The powers not delegated to the United States by the Constitution, nor prohibited by it to the States, are reserved to the States respectively, or to the people.

Additional Amendments

Amendment 11

The Judicial power of the United States shall not be construed to extend to any suit in law or equity, commenced or prosecuted against one of the United States by Citizens of another State, or by Citizens or Subjects of any Foreign State.

Amendment 12

The Electors shall meet in their respective states, and vote by ballot for President and Vice-President, one of whom, at least, shall not be an inhabitant of the same state with themselves; they shall name in their ballots the person voted for as President, and in distinct ballots the person voted for as Vice-President, and they shall make distinct lists of all persons voted for as President, and of all persons voted for as Vice-President and of the number of votes for each, which lists they shall sign and certify, and transmit sealed to the seat of the government of the United States, directed to the President of the Senate;

The President of the Senate shall, in the presence of the Senate and House of Representatives, open all the certificates and the votes shall then be counted;

The person having the greatest Number of votes for President, shall be the President, if such number be a majority of the whole number of Electors appointed; and if no person have such majority, then from the persons having the highest numbers not exceeding three on the list of those voted for as President, the House of Representatives shall choose immediately, by ballot, the President. But in choosing the President, the votes shall be taken by states, the representation from each state having one vote; a quorum for this purpose shall consist of a member or members from two-thirds of the states, and a majority of all the states shall be necessary to a choice. And if the House of Representatives shall not choose a President whenever the right of choice shall devolve upon them, before the fourth day of March next following, then the Vice-President shall act as President, as in the case of the death or other constitutional disability of the President.

The person having the greatest number of votes as Vice-President, shall be the Vice-President, if such number be a majority of the whole number of Electors appointed, and if no person have a majority, then from the two highest numbers on the list, the Senate shall choose the Vice-President; a quorum for the purpose shall consist of two-thirds of the whole number of Senators, and a majority of the whole number shall be necessary to a choice. But no person constitutionally ineligible to the office of President shall be eligible to that of Vice-President of the United States.

Amendment 13

1. Neither slavery nor involuntary servitude, except as a punishment for crime whereof the party shall have been duly convicted, shall exist within the United States, or any place subject to their jurisdiction.

2. Congress shall have power to enforce this article by appropriate legislation.

Amendment 14

1. All persons born or naturalized in the United States, and subject to the jurisdiction thereof, are citizens of the United States and of the State wherein they reside. No State shall make or enforce any law which shall abridge the privileges or immunities of citizens of the United States; nor shall any State deprive any person of life, liberty, or property, without due process of law; nor deny to any person within its jurisdiction the equal protection of the laws.

2. Representatives shall be apportioned among the several States according to their respective numbers, counting the whole number of persons in each State, excluding Indians not taxed. But when the right to vote at any election for the choice of electors for President and Vice-President of the United States, Representatives in Congress, the Executive and Judicial officers of a State, or the members of the Legislature thereof, is denied to any of the male inhabitants of such State, being twenty-one years of age, and citizens of the United States, or in any way abridged, except for participation in rebellion, or other crime, the basis of representation therein shall be reduced in the proportion which the number of such male citizens shall bear to the

whole number of male citizens twenty-one years of age in such State.

3. No person shall be a Senator or Representative in Congress, or elector of President and Vice-President, or hold any office, civil or military, under the United States, or under any State, who, having previously taken an oath, as a member of Congress, or as an officer of the United States, or as a member of any State legislature, or as an executive or judicial officer of any State, to support the Constitution of the United States, shall have engaged in insurrection or rebellion against the same, or given aid or comfort to the enemies thereof. But Congress may by a vote of two-thirds of each House, remove such disability.

4. The validity of the public debt of the United States, authorized by law, including debts incurred for payment of pensions and bounties for services in suppressing insurrection or rebellion, shall not be questioned. But neither the United States nor any State shall assume or pay any debt or obligation incurred in aid of insurrection or rebellion against the United States, or any claim for the loss or emancipation of any slave; but all such debts, obligations and claims shall be held illegal and void.

5. The Congress shall have power to enforce, by appropriate legislation, the provisions of this article.

Amendment 15
1. The right of citizens of the United States to vote shall not be denied or abridged by the United States or by any State on account of race, color, or previous condition of servitude.

2. The Congress shall have power to enforce this article by appropriate legislation.

Amendment 16
The Congress shall have power to lay and collect taxes on incomes, from whatever source derived, without apportionment among the several States, and without regard to any census or enumeration.

Amendment 17
The Senate of the United States shall be composed of two Senators from each State, elected by the people thereof, for six years; and each Senator shall have one vote. The electors in each State shall have the qualifications requisite for electors of the most numerous branch of the State legislatures.

When vacancies happen in the representation of any State in the Senate, the executive authority of such State shall issue writs of election to fill such vacancies: Provided, That the legislature of any State may empower the

Signing Their Rights Away

executive thereof to make temporary appointments until the people fill the vacancies by election as the legislature may direct.

This amendment shall not be so construed as to affect the election or term of any Senator chosen before it becomes valid as part of the Constitution.

Amendment 18

1. After one year from the ratification of this article the manufacture, sale, or transportation of intoxicating liquors within, the importation thereof into, or the exportation thereof from the United States and all territory subject to the jurisdiction thereof for beverage purposes is hereby prohibited.

2. The Congress and the several States shall have concurrent power to enforce this article by appropriate legislation.

3. This article shall be inoperative unless it shall have been ratified as an amendment to the Constitution by the legislatures of the several States, as provided in the Constitution, within seven years from the date of the submission hereof to the States by the Congress.

Amendment 19

The right of citizens of the United States to vote shall not be denied or abridged by the United States or by any State on account of sex.

Congress shall have power to enforce this article by appropriate legislation.

Amendment 20

1. The terms of the President and Vice President shall end at noon on the 20th day of January, and the terms of Senators and Representatives at noon on the 3d day of January, of the years in which such terms would have ended if this article had not been ratified; and the terms of their successors shall then begin.

2. The Congress shall assemble at least once in every year, and such meeting shall begin at noon on the 3d day of January, unless they shall by law appoint a different day.

3. If, at the time fixed for the beginning of the term of the President, the President elect shall have died, the Vice President elect shall become President. If a President shall not have been chosen before the time fixed for the beginning of his term, or if the President elect shall have failed to qualify, then the Vice President elect shall act as President until a President shall have qualified; and the Congress may by law provide for the case wherein neither a President elect nor a Vice President elect shall have qualified, declaring who shall then act as President, or the manner in which one who is to act shall be selected,

and such person shall act accordingly until a President or Vice President shall have qualified.

4. The Congress may by law provide for the case of the death of any of the persons from whom the House of Representatives may choose a President whenever the right of choice shall have devolved upon them, and for the case of the death of any of the persons from whom the Senate may choose a Vice President whenever the right of choice shall have devolved upon them.

5. Sections 1 and 2 shall take effect on the 15th day of October following the ratification of this article.

6. This article shall be inoperative unless it shall have been ratified as an amendment to the Constitution by the legislatures of three-fourths of the several States within seven years from the date of its submission.

Amendment 21

1. The eighteenth article of amendment to the Constitution of the United States is hereby repealed.

2. The transportation or importation into any State, Territory, or possession of the United States for delivery or use therein of intoxicating liquors, in violation of the laws thereof, is hereby prohibited.

3. The article shall be inoperative unless it shall have been ratified as an amendment to the Constitution by conventions in the several States, as provided in the Constitution, within seven years from the date of the submission hereof to the States by the Congress.

Amendment 22

1. No person shall be elected to the office of the President more than twice, and no person who has held the office of President, or acted as President, for more than two years of a term to which some other person was elected President shall be elected to the office of the President more than once. But this Article shall not apply to any person holding the office of President, when this Article was proposed by the Congress, and shall not prevent any person who may be holding the office of President, or acting as President, during the term within which this Article becomes operative from holding the office of President or acting as President during the remainder of such term.

2. This article shall be inoperative unless it shall have been ratified as an amendment to the Constitution by the legislatures of three-fourths of the several States within seven years from the date of its submission to the States by the Congress.

Signing Their Rights Away

Amendment 23

1. The District constituting the seat of Government of the United States shall appoint in such manner as the Congress may direct:

A number of electors of President and Vice President equal to the whole number of Senators and Representatives in Congress to which the District would be entitled if it were a State, but in no event more than the least populous State; they shall be in addition to those appointed by the States, but they shall be considered, for the purposes of the election of President and Vice President, to be electors appointed by a State; and they shall meet in the District and perform such duties as provided by the twelfth article of amendment.

2. The Congress shall have power to enforce this article by appropriate legislation.

Amendment 24

1. The right of citizens of the United States to vote in any primary or other election for President or Vice President, for electors for President or Vice President, or for Senator or Representative in Congress, shall not be denied or abridged by the United States or any State by reason of failure to pay poll tax or other tax.

2. The Congress shall have power to enforce this article by appropriate legislation.

Amendment 25

1. In case of the removal of the President from office or of his death or resignation, the Vice President shall become President.

2. Whenever there is a vacancy in the office of the Vice President, the President shall nominate a Vice President who shall take office upon confirmation by a majority vote of both Houses of Congress.

3. Whenever the President transmits to the President pro tempore of the Senate and the Speaker of the House of Representatives his written declaration that he is unable to discharge the powers and duties of his office, and until he transmits to them a written declaration to the contrary, such powers and duties shall be discharged by the Vice President as Acting President.

4. Whenever the Vice President and a majority of either the principal officers of the executive departments or of such other body as Congress may by law provide, transmit to the President pro tempore of the Senate and the Speaker of the House of Representatives their written declaration that the President is unable to discharge the powers and duties of his office, the

Vice President shall immediately assume the powers and duties of the office as Acting President.

Thereafter, when the President transmits to the President pro tempore of the Senate and the Speaker of the House of Representatives his written declaration that no inability exists, he shall resume the powers and duties of his office unless the Vice President and a majority of either the principal officers of the executive department or of such other body as Congress may by law provide, transmit within four days to the President pro tempore of the Senate and the Speaker of the House of Representatives their written declaration that the President is unable to discharge the powers and duties of his office. Thereupon Congress shall decide the issue, assembling within forty-eight hours for that purpose if not in session. If the Congress, within twenty-one days after receipt of the latter written declaration, or, if Congress is not in session, within twenty-one days after Congress is required to assemble, determines by two-thirds vote of both Houses that the President is unable to discharge the powers and duties of his office, the Vice President shall continue to discharge the same as Acting President; otherwise, the President shall resume the powers and duties of his office.

Amendment 26

1. The right of citizens of the United States, who are eighteen years of age or older, to vote shall not be denied or abridged by the United States or by any State on account of age.

2. The Congress shall have power to enforce this article by appropriate legislation.

Amendment 27

No law, varying the compensation for the services of the Senators and Representatives, shall take effect, until an election of Representatives shall have intervened.

Appendix II.

A Constitutional Miscellany

★ ★

Here is an assortment of odd facts about the United States Constitution. How is it preserved? Who's responsible for all the fancy calligraphy? Who is William Jackson and why is his name buried in the far left corner of the document? We've got all the answers right here.

Preserving the Constitution

When Americans love something, they love it to death—which might explain why the original copy of the Declaration of Independence has faded to the point that it is barely legible. The U.S. Constitution, on the other hand, is in much better shape and can still be read fairly easily.

The disparity in the conditions of the two documents owes much to the way they were preserved (or not) over the years. Created during wartime, the Declaration traveled up and down the East Coast of the United States to protect it from marauding armies. It was manhandled at every turn. After the War of 1812, the Declaration was displayed on a wall and exposed to the damaging rays of the sun. Meanwhile, the Constitution napped cozily in a steel box, virtually forgotten. Many people felt it just wasn't as important or as venerable as the Declaration—and this wrongheaded thinking saved it for posterity.

In 1952 both the Declaration and the Constitution went on display in a special shrine built for them within the National Archives, locked permanently in glass cases filled with helium. Over time, however, the cases deteriorated, threatening the documents inside. So in 2001, conservators at the archives embarked on an ambitious program to rescue the documents with space-age technology.

Today all three Charters of Freedom—the Declaration of Independence, the Constitution, and the Bill of Rights—are preserved in titanium cases fitted with special glass that can withstand bombs, bullets, hurricanes, and the most vitriolic of filibusters. The panes shield the documents from ultraviolet light while allowing tourists to see through to read the text. The temperature inside the cases is kept at about 67°F (19°C), and the atmosphere contains not oxygen but humidified argon. The touch of moisture prevents the documents from becoming too brittle.

The Penman of the Constitution

If you've ever inspected the words "We the People" on the original Constitution, you've probably marveled at the skill with which the letters have been perfectly formed. The man who copied the entire Constitution by hand in flawless calligraphy is Jacob Shallus, a clerk about thirty-seven years old. Born to a Dutch family who had immigrated to Pennsylvania, Shallus served in the Revolutionary War, working as a quartermaster, or supplier. No one knows when he realized his gift for exquisite penmanship, but after the war he began working as a clerk in the Pennsylvania Assembly, the state's lawmaking body. He worked in the same building in which the delegates met and was, therefore, the most logical scribe for the job.

Shallus had to work quickly. He was handed the final text for the Constitution on Friday, September 15, 1787, and was requested to turn in a finished copy on Monday, September 17.

Considering it was a weekend, he possibly worked at home, though that's unlikely since he needed easy access to equipment. He used quill pens and ink, probably of his own manufacture; the parchment, which is made of stretched calf skin, was likely bought from a local supplier. To help keep the words and letters even, he used a straight edge to mark faint lines on the parchment, which are still visible on the originals (and can be seen in high-resolution images available on the National Archives' website). If he made a mistake, he would have been forced to scrape off the ink with a knife and rewrite the offending word or letter. In fact, some errors did work their way into the final document. Shallus listed the ones he spotted in a small errata paragraph, visible at the bottom of the fourth page of the document. But the Constitution contains others that Shallus did not catch, such as odd misspellings and punctuation issues that he may have copied from the original papers. Rules for grammar and style varied widely in the eighteenth century, and it was not unusual for people to spell even their own names two different ways in a single document.

Come Monday, the delegates had the finished document ready to be signed, and Shallus, penman of the State House, pocketed $30 for his moonlighting gig, an amount equivalent to more than $700 in today's money. Not bad for a weekend's work, but apparently not enough to keep Shallus from running into financial trouble. Within a year, he was facing a stay in a debtors' prison, only barely managing to avert that disaster. When he died, in 1796, he was just forty-six years old.

Twentieth-century scholars were unaware of Shallus until 1937, the 150th anniversary of the Constitution, when a little detective work revealed his small but vital contribution to the history of the United States.

William Jackson: The Fortieth Signer

The bottom far-left corner of the Constitution displays a signature that does not belong to any of the official delegates at the Constitutional Convention. It reads: "Attest William Jackson Secretary."

Sometimes described as the fortieth signer—though he did not sign as a representative of any state—Jackson was born in 1759 on the border between England and Scotland. After his parents died, he was sent to Charleston, South Carolina, to be raised by a family friend.

During the Revolutionary War, Jackson joined the fighting in South Carolina, first as a cadet and eventually achieving the rank of major. In 1780, during the siege of Charleston, he was captured and paroled to Philadelphia; he was later released in a prisoner exchange. He then served as secretary to Lieutenant Colonel John Laurens, who was Washington's aide, traveling with him to France to orchestrate the shipping of supplies for the war. Once back in Philadelphia, Jackson was made assistant secretary at war to Major General Benjamin Lincoln, for whom he had served in the south.

After the war, Jackson tried business and law in Philadelphia. He lobbied hard for the secretarial job at the Constitutional Convention and almost didn't get it. On the first day of the convention, signer James Wilson suggested Temple Franklin, Benjamin Franklin's grandson, for the post. Most folks didn't care for Temple, who was viewed as a narcissistic fashion plate and playboy who had already fathered a child out of wedlock with a married woman. The popular (and perhaps Puritan-inspired) perception was that Temple's time in France with Grandpa Franklin— also known for his love of the ladies—had rendered the boy's character a little too effetely French. Jackson, however, had connected with Alexander Hamilton during the war. Hamilton vouched for Jackson, whom he thought would be a good fit for the post and whose military service he found impressive.

But Jackson, it must be said, proved to be a weak link. John Quincy Adams, while serving as secretary of state, complained that Jackson's convention notes were an illegible mess; his records were so sparse, in fact, as to be distinctly unhelpful. For instance, Jackson made no entries on September 17, the day of the signing. On top of this omission, he had thrown away, according to Adams, all the "loose scraps of paper" and other notes given to him by the delegates. In his defense, he may have done so to follow the delegates' instructions to keep only the official journal and toss all else. In this sense, Jackson probably did his duty by safeguarding convention secrets. But, as a result, historians have been forced to rely solely upon the notes taken by James Madison. As we've learned

Signing Their Rights Away

from the tale of the Pinckney Plan, Madison may not have been the most impartial recorder of events. Imagine all the juicy tidbits upon which ravenous historians could feast today if we still had the papers that Jackson burnt, tossed, or shredded. Delicious scandal! Scrumptious fights! Delectable power plays! Alas, we are left only with Madison's version.

Jackson became Washington's secretary during the latter's presidency, but financial difficulties caused him to resign in 1791. He then became a businessman and a lawyer and was appointed surveyor of customs for the port of Philadelphia. He also served more than twenty-five years as national secretary for the Society of the Cincinnati, an organization made up of Continental Army veterans.

William Jackson's grave in Christ Church Burial Ground in Philadelphia had grown so dilapidated that for many years no one even knew the resting place belonged to him. Only recently did tour guides at the site investigate the church's records and deduce that the person buried under the broken and poorly repaired stone was the convention's unremarkable secretary.

Will the Real Constitution Printer Please Stand Up?

We know who signed it, and we know the man responsible for the fancy handwriting—but who *printed* the first public copies of the Constitution?

The honor has historically gone to the printing team of David C. Claypoole and John Dunlap, better known for printing the "Dunlap Broadside," the first typeset version of the Declaration of Independence. For about two hundred years, these two men have been credited with printing the first public copy of the Constitution as well, which appeared in their Philadelphia paper, *The Pennsylvania Packet,* even though four other papers published the Constitution on that same day. New evidence has led some scholars to believe that someone else might have scooped them all.

Here's the time line: On Friday, September 15, the convention delegates ordered an engrossed copy of the Constitution from penman Jacob Shallus, and five hundred plain printed copies of the text from Dunlap and Claypoole, which were to be widely distributed so that Congress and the states could be informed of what the delegates in Philadelphia had created. The engrossed and other copies were needed by Monday, September 17, at which point the delegates would sign the engrossed copy. The original and the other five hundred copies would be sent to New York, where Congress awaited the results of the convention.

Shallus and Dunlap and Claypoole met their deadlines, but the delegates wanted to make some pesky last-minute changes, and everything had to be ready in time for the 10 a.m. stagecoach to New York City on the morning of September 18. The changes were made to the engrossed copy, but the five hundred printed copies had to be tossed. Dunlap and Claypoole printed a quickie six-page version of the new document, and that broadside (eleven are known to exist) went on to serve as the source document for all other printings.

So when was the new Constitution released to the rest of the world? Enter Robert Smith, a printer who had worked for Dunlap and Claypoole's *Pennsylvania Packet* in 1786 and launched *The Evening Chronicle* the next year. In 2001, a copy of a broadside titled *Plan of the New Federal Government* and dated September 17, 1787, was found with Smith's name in plain view. It is believed by some historians to have been printed as an insert in the September 18 edition of *The Evening Chronicle*, but no complete copy of that edition of the paper exists—only the broadside itself.

Was there a hot-off-the-printing-press leaked copy? Errors in Smith's version and other evidence point to a hasty printing. An infantry paymaster in Philadelphia wrote in his diary about seeing a printed version of the Constitution as early as September 18. But five Philadelphia papers—including *The Pennsylvania Packet*—published the Constitution on September 19, a day *after* the printing to which the paymaster refers, leading researchers to believe that Smith's broadside was the only one the paymaster could have seen. If this recent evidence is true, it would make for quite the revolutionary scoop. Somehow Smith got hold of the document and set it in type before anyone else could, including his old boss. Despite his valiant, Jimmy Olsen–type efforts, Smith's *Chronicle* went out of business in November 1787. Today only twenty-five copies of the September 19, 1787, edition of *The Pennsylvania Packet* are known to exist, and only one Smith broadside is known to exist. It was sold at auction in 2006 for $160,000 and turned for sale shortly after for $335,000.

Who Signed the Bill of Rights?

Most Americans know more about the Bill of Rights, a k a the first ten amendments to the Constitution, than they do about the Constitution itself—and for good reason. The Bill of Rights sets forth the terms of individual liberties enjoyed by Americans, such as freedom of speech, freedom of religion, and so on. But this beloved document was not part of the original four pages signed by the delegates on September 17, 1787, much to the dismay and outright anger of those who signed and many more who did not.

As soon as the Constitution went into effect and the first U.S. Congress met, the Bill of Rights was at the top of the agenda. Hoping to stave off another Constitutional Convention, James Madison drafted and presented seventeen proposed amendments in the first few months the new Congress was operational under the Constitution. This list was whittled down to twelve amendments, which President Washington sent to the states for ratification. The first two, concerning Congressional issues, were not ratified. But the remaining ones became the first ten amendments by 1791.

The copy preserved by the National Archives in the rotunda, with the Declaration of Independence and the Constitution, is signed by four men: John Adams, then vice president of the United States; Frederick Augustus Muhlenberg, speaker of the House of Representatives; John Beckley, clerk of the House of Representatives; and Samuel A. Otis, secretary of the Senate.

By the Numbers

A small selection of trivia, tidbits, and important numbers from the Constitutional Convention of 1787.

• The oldest signer was Ben Franklin, age 81. He was also the first signer to die.

• The youngest signer was New Jersey's Jonathan Dayton, age 26.

• The document was written in approximately 100 days.

• The youngest signer to die was Richard Dobbs Spaight, age 44.

• The longest-lived signer was William Samuel Johnson, age 92.

• The last signer to die was James Madison, in 1836.

• The number of signers who were bachelors: 3. (Daniel of St. Thomas Jenifer, Nicholas Gilman, Abraham Baldwin)

• The number of men invited to attend the Constitutional Convention: 74.

• The number who attended: 55.

• The number who signed: 39, though technically 38. (George Read acted as John Dickinson's proxy.)

• Besides Dickinson, the number of men who left the convention for various reasons and never signed: 13.

- The number of men who stayed till the end but refused to sign: 3 (Elbridge Gerry, Edmund Randolph, and George Mason)
- Number of states attending: 12 (Rhode Island declined.)
- Number of states needed to ratify before the Constitution was put into play, a presidential election could be held, and the first Congress could be selected: 9.

They Came, They Saw, They Didn't Sign

Although fifty-five men attended the Constitutional Convention, only thirty-nine put their names to the document. What happened to the other sixteen? Each had reasons for omitting his name. Some stayed until the very last day but refused to sign because they were angry about what the document did or did not achieve. Others left during the process because they objected to the proceedings or they had business, family matters, or pressing concerns elsewhere that needed their attention. (Attendance wasn't mandatory.) Here's what we know about the would-be signers.

Massachusetts

Elbridge Gerry: This stammering delegate, a signer of the Declaration of Independence who became the rascally father of gerrymandering, stayed to the end but refused to sign because the final document lacked a Bill of Rights. He thought the Constitution would lead to civil war if ratified.

Caleb Strong: This wealthy country lawyer liked the Constitution but left because of a family illness.

Connecticut

Oliver Ellsworth: This intelligent lawyer approved of the Constitution but left the convention because of family obligations. He later served as the nation's third chief justice.

New York

John Lansing Jr.: This wealthy patrician lawyer from Albany was appointed to block Alexander Hamilton's efforts to form a strong central government. Annoyed by the proceedings, he left the convention on July 10 and never returned. Years later, at age seventy-five, he left a Manhattan hotel to go mail a letter and was never seen again. He was presumed murdered.

Robert Yates: Also sent to block Hamilton, this New York state judge left on July 10 as well, saying he had not been authorized to go beyond a revision of the Articles of Confederation. Once wealthy, he died poor.

New Jersey

William Churchill Houston: This delegate was a highly paid public servant working for the state. He was ill during convention, left, and later died of tuberculosis.

Maryland

John Francis Mercer: This wealthy lawyer and planter left early, objecting to the Constitution on the grounds that it lacked a Bill of Rights and was not democratic enough.

Luther Martin: This hard-drinking, slovenly Baltimore attorney is remembered for his inebriated, six-hour speech in defense of the equal voting rights of states. He opposed the Constitution for the same reasons as Mercer. Both men fought against the document at their state's ratifying convention.

Virginia

Edmund Randolph: Virginia's governor at the time of the convention, he's best known for having presented the Virginia Plan. He stayed to the end but objected to the Constitution, refused to sign, and predicted that nothing but chaos would come of it. He later changed his mind and supported it.

George Mason: The man who wrote the Virginia document that greatly influenced Jefferson's text of the Declaration of Independence, Mason distrusted central government. He stayed to the very end but refused to sign the Constitution and fought its ratification.

George Wythe: A signer of the Declaration of Independence and Jefferson's mentor, he approved of the Constitution and supported its ratification. He left the convention because his wife was sick. He was later poisoned to death by his grand-nephew.

James McClurg: It's believed this doctor would have supported the Constitution, but he left because he was too intimidated by the level of the discussion and didn't fit in.

North Carolina

Alexander Martin: This once and future governor of North Carolina left in August because he didn't like the Constitution. He later supported its ratification on the state level.

William Richardson Davie: This lawyer and former military officer left early because of family illness and later supported the document's ratification.

Georgia

William Pierce: Famous for the character sketches he penned of all the delegates, this struggling merchant left to tend to some troubling business issues back home. He died about two years after the convention.

William Houstoun: This delegate, a lawyer, planter, and namesake of New York City's famous Houston Street (pronounced *HOW-stin*), left early, opposing the Constitution because he supported only a revision of the Articles of Confederation.

Immigrant Signers

Only seven of the Constitution signers were immigrants. Those born outside the original thirteen colonies were:

• Pierce Butler of South Carolina: Born County Carlow, Ireland, 1744

• Thomas FitzSimons of Pennsylvania: Born County Wexford, Ireland, 1741

• James McHenry of Maryland: Born Country Antrim, Ireland, 1753

• William Paterson of New Jersey: Born County Antrim, Ireland, 1745

• Robert Morris of Pennsylvania: Born Liverpool, England, 1734

• James Wilson of Pennsylvania: Born Carskerdo, Scotland, 1742

• Alexander Hamilton of New York: Born Charlestown, Nevis, British West Indies, 1755

* * * * * * * * * * * * *

Signing Their Rights Away

Selected Bibliography

Barefoot, Daniel W. *Touring the Backroads of North Carolina's Lower Coast*. Winston-Salem, NC: John F. Blair, 1995.

Beard, Charles A. *An Economic Interpretation of the Constitution of the United States*. New York: The Free Press, 1986.

Beeman, Richard. *Plain, Honest Men: The Making of the American Constitution*. New York: Random House, 2009.

Bell, Robert R. *The Philadelphia Lawyer: A History, 1735–1945*. Selinsgrove, PA: Susquehanna University Press, 1992.

Berkin, Carol. *A Brilliant Solution: Inventing the American Constitution*. New York: Harvest/Harcourt, 2002.

Binney, Horace. *The Leaders of the Old Bar of Philadelphia*. Philadelphia: C. Sherman & Son, 1859.

Bowen, Catherine Drinker. *Miracle at Philadelphia: The Story of the Constitutional Convention, May to September 1787*. New York: Back Bay Books/Little, Brown, 1966.

Channing, Edward. *A History of the United States, Volume III: The American Revolution, 1761–1789*. New York: Macmillan, 1912.

Collier, Christopher, and James Lincoln Collier. *Decision in Philadelphia: The Constitutional Convention of 1787*. New York: Ballantine Books, 1986.

Campbell, Rev. William W. *The Life and Character of Jacob Broom*. Wilmington: Historical Society of Delaware, 1909.

Ferris, Robert G. and James H. Charleton. *The Signers of the Constitution*. Arlington, VA: Interpretive Publications, 1986.

Ford, Paul Leicester, ed. *The Writings of John Dickinson: Political Writings, 1764–1774*, Volume 1. Philadelphia: Publication Fund of the Historical Society of Pennsylvania, 1895.

Fradin, Dennis Brindell. *The Founders: The 39 Stories behind the U.S. Constitution*. New York: Walker & Co., 2005.

Haw, James. *John & Edward Rutledge of South Carolina.* Athens: University of Georgia Press, 1997.

Hess, Stephen. *America's Political Dynasties.* New Brunswick, NJ: Transaction Publishers, 1997.

Hosack, David. *A Biographical Memoir of Hugh Williamson, MD, LLD.* New York: C. S. Van Winkle, 1820.

King, Charles R., ed. *The Life and Correspondence of Rufus King.* Vol. 1, 1755–1794. New York: G. P. Putnam's Sons, 1894.

Knight, Lucian Lamar. *Memorials of Dixie-land: Orations, Essays, Sketches, and Poems on Topics Historical, Commemorative, Literary, and Patriotic.* Atlanta: Byra Printing, 1919.

Lidz, Maggie. *The du Ponts: Houses and Gardens in the Brandywine, 1900–1951.* New York: Acanthus Press, 2009

Linn, John B., and William H. Eagle. *Papers Relating to What Is Known as the Whiskey Rebellion in Western Pennsylvania, 1794.* Pennsylvania Archives, Second Series, vol. IV. Harrisburg: E. K. Meyers, 1890.

Macdonald, Forrest. *We the People: The Economic Origins of the Constitution.* New Brunswick, NJ: Transaction Publishers, 1992.

Maxwell, William. *The Virginia Historical Register, and Literary Companion,* vols. 5–6, Virginia Historical Society. Richmond: MacFarlane & Fergusson, 1852.

Monk, Linda R. *The Words We Live By: Your Annotated Guide to the Constitution.* New York: Stonesong Press, 2003.

Morris, Robert, Elizabeth M. Nuxoll, et al., eds. *The Papers of Robert Morris, 1781–1784: January 1–October 30, 1784.* Pittsburgh: University of Pittsburgh Press, 1999.

Morton, Joseph C. *Shapers of the Great Debate at the Constitutional Convention of 1787: A Biographical Dictionary.* Westport, CT: Greenwood Press, 2006.

Quinn, Bro. C. Edward. *The Signers of the Constitution.* Bronx, NY: Bronx Historical Society, 1987.

Rakove, Jack N. *Original Meanings: Politics and Ideas in the Making of the Constitution.* New York: Vintage Books, 1997.

Ratzlaff, Robert K. *John Rutledge Jr.: South Carolina Federalist, 1766–1819.* Manchester, NH: Ayer Publishing, 1982

Read, William Thompson. *Life and Correspondence of George Read: A Signer of the Declaration of Independence.* Philadelphia: J. B. Lippincott, 1870.

Simpson, Philip. *The Lives of Eminent Philadelphians, Now Deceased, Collected from Original and Authentic Sources.* Philadelphia: William Brotherhead, 1859.

Steiner, Bernard Christian. *The Life and Correspondence of James McHenry.* Cleveland, OH: Burrows Brothers, 1907.

Stellwagen, Thomas C., ed. *Historical and Biographical Papers, Vol. III.* Wilmington: Historical Society of Delaware, 1897.

Stewart, David O. *The Summer of 1787: The Men Who Invented the Constitution.* New York: Simon & Schuster, 2007.

Vile, John R. *The Constitutional Convention of 1787: A Comprehensive Encyclopedia of America's Founding, Vol. 2.* Santa Barbara, CA: ABC-CLIO, 2005.

Whitney, David C. *Founders of Freedom in America: Lives of the Men Who Signed the Constitution of the United States and So Helped Establish the United States of America.* Chicago: J. G. Ferguson, 1965.

Williams, Selma R. *The Fifty-Five Fathers.* New York: Dodd, Mead, 1970.

Wright, Robert K., Jr., and Morris J. MacGregor Jr. *Soldier-Statesmen of the Constitution.* Washington, D.C.: Center of Military History, United States, Army, 1987

Index

and Hugh Williamson, 182–83
and James Wilson, 106
U.S. Constitution, 17, 102, 113,
  242
Franklin, Temple, 238
Franklin, William, 62, 65, 69
French, Susanna, 61
French and Indian War, 28, 153
French Revolution, 113, 158
Friendly Sons of Saint Patrick, 97

Galloway, Joseph, 119
Gates, Horatio, 85, 173
Georgia
  Abraham Baldwin, 210–13, 242
  Chisholm v. Georgia, 102-103
  William Few, 206–9, 212
  William Houstoun, 212, 245
  See also Pierce, William
Gerry, Elbridge, 35, 194, 242, 243
Gilman, John Taylor, 30
Gilman, Nicholas, 26, 28–30, 242
Gorham, Nathaniel, 32–35, 99, 131
Grainger, Mary, 173
Gray, Hannah, 108
Great Britain
  Ambassador Rufus King, 38, 39
  arming Native Americans, 10
  Franklin as agent of Pennsylvania,
    79–80
  French and Indian War, 28, 153
  government as model, 54
  Treaty of Paris, 18
  War of 1812, 138, 141, 168–69,
    236
  See also Revolutionary War
Great Compromise, 81–82
  drafters, 16, 49, 70, 124
  opponents, 167
  supporters, 44, 63, 66, 73, 98,
    121
Grimké, Elizabeth, 187
Gwinnett, Button, 180

Hamilton, Alexander, 52–57, 245
  Annapolis Convention, 166
  Articles of Confederation, 11,
    165–66
  Constitutional Convention, 112,
    131–32, 238
  duel, 180

Federalist Papers, 17, 167
financial system, 89, 90, 121, 148,
  157
and George Washington, 157
and Rufus King, 38
and William Livingston, 62
and James McHenry, 140–41
Revolutionary War, 73, 139
Secretary of the Treasury, 35, 71
Hartwell, Elizabeth, 47
Harvard College, 37, 42
Henry, Patrick, 11, 114, 161–63,
  166–67
Holmes v. Walton, 65–66
Hopkins, Stephen, 83
Houston, William Churchill, 243
Houstoun, William, 212, 245
Howard, John Eager, 39
Hylton v. United States, 103

immigrant signers, 245
  Pierce Butler, 201–202
  Thomas FitzSimons, 96
  James McHenry, 138–39
  William Paterson, 68
  James Wilson, 104–5
  See also Hamilton, Alexander;
    Morris, Robert
impeachment, 103, 175–76
Ingersoll, Jared, 100–103, 176
Insurance Company of North
  America, 99
Iredell, James, 108

Jackson, Andrew, 169, 175
Jackson, William, 198, 238–39
Jay, John, 17, 107, 110, 167, 189–90
Jay Treaty, 190, 199
Jefferson, Thomas, 26, 39, 47
  and Aaron Burr, 74–75
  Constitutional Convention, 48,
    183–84
  currency, 111
  Declaration on the Causes and
    Necessity of Taking Up Arms,
    128
  Democratic-Republican Party, 168
  elections, 114
  and George Washington, 157–58
  governor, 166
  on John Dickinson, 129

Signing Their Rights Away

Signing Their Rights Away

Signing Their Rights Away

Acknowledgments

★ ★

The U.S. Constitution was written by fifty-five men in one hundred days. This book had just two authors, and thus it took much longer. We are indebted to quite a few people for making it happen. This book would not have been possible without the encouragement and thoughtfulness of our editor, Jason Rekulak, and his colleagues, who include David Borgenicht, Brett Cohen, Melissa Monachello, and Eric Smith. Copy editor Mary Ellen Wilson whipped the prose, "olde" and otherwise, into shape. Designer Katie Hatz created a beautiful volume and keepsake. We are honored to have Robert Carter's amazing illustrations grace this volume. Lastly, we must thank our family, friends, and colleagues who patiently endured trips to graveyards, libraries, and historic sites or, worse yet, had to listen to overly enthusiastic verbal descriptions and view photos pertaining to those trips undertaken during the writing of this book. Though most of these people contributed in some way to this project and its predecessor, we are solely responsible for any errors and omissions. You may direct questions or comments to our website: signingtheirlivesaway.com.

★ ★ ★ ★ ★ ★ ★ ★ ★ ★ ★ ★